EYEWITNESS ON ALCATRAZ

*Life on THE ROCK as told by
the Guards, Families & Prisoners*

EYEWITNESS ON ALCATRAZ

*Life on THE ROCK as told by
the Guards, Families & Prisoners*

by
Jolene Babyak

Ariel Vamp Press
Berkeley, California

INTRODUCTION & ACKNOWLEDGMENT

In a collection of critical essays entitled *Under the Sign of Saturn,* Susan Sontag suggested that a written piece, having veracity, emotional power and subtlety, and being written from a system of outrage, should at once sum up and oppose one's age. This has been my goal in writing about Alcatraz and my father's involvement there during one of the most pivotal times of American prison history.

Alcatraz emerged in the 1930s at a time of economic depression, aggressive lawlessness and unchecked media glorification of crime and criminals. The government and the media in 1934 heralded it as *the* escape-proof prison where only the worst prisoners would be sent, and in which the rules would be so strict as to break mens' spirits. Thereafter official news from Alcatraz was withheld and the only stories to emerge were from sensational murder trials and from ex-prisoners. Thus, the myth of Alcatraz as a place of brutality grew. The prison closed twenty–nine years later, an old and decrepit facility, victim of its own myth, blemished by its final escape attempts and the changing attitudes of federal prison management.

To claim that it was a brutal prison is too simple. To make a definitive statement about treatment there is reckless, because throughout the years four wardens ruled, each with vastly different management styles and temperaments, in eras as different as those of Presidents Herbert C. Hoover in the 1930s and John F. Kennedy in the 1960s.

Moreover, it should come as no surprise that many prisoners found when they left that they preferred life on "The Rock," with one man to a cell and less than three hundred prisoners, than to living in prison populations of fifteen hundred, or three or five thousand men like other federal and state penitentiaries.

Therein lies the gray area I've narrated here. My purpose has been to interpret and comment on the statements of the more than sixty people I've interviewed, writing from my own system of outrage, at once summing up and opposing the Alcatraz era. It's an effort, as Sontag also said, to "be true, and not just interesting."

I could have never written this book without a significant amount of work by my father, Arthur M. Dollison, on his own memories of nine years of working on Alcatraz. His sense of history, follow through and generosity in allowing me to interpret what was ultimately his subject showed more love than I ever knew.

And, I would like to thank the following people: Colleen Collins, Operations Supervisor, Rich Weideman, Supervisory Park Ranger, and Rex Norman, Park Ranger, Golden Gate National Recreation Area, National Park Service; Stephen A. Haller, Historian, National Maritime Museum; Irene Stachura, Librarian, J. Porter Shaw Library, National Maritime Museum; John Brunner, who printed many of the photographs; Tom Averill and Jeff Goudie, whose critical comments, edification and sincere dedication to my project was of immeasurable help; Nan Harper, Tresa Hill, Don Mayberger, Linda "Sam" Haskins, Kathy Hoggard, Jane Nichols, Tonda Rush, Polly Pettit-Dowling, Molly Laflin, Robert and Nancy Marshall, Vickie Randel and all the others originally from Lawrence, Kansas; Cirla Dallos, Lacy Curtis-Ward, and Kathy Laurin; Nancy Olmsted, Ken Fox, and David Bullen; Ruth Teiser, who was a wonderful inspiration to me; my brother, Philip F. Dollison, his wife, Ann, and my sister, Corinne Dollison Edwards, whose generosity, financial support and interest were of invaluable help. Finally, without the guidance, interest and encouragement of the Golden Gate National Parks Association, I wouldn't have continued to explore more themes.

Marla Eisenberg, naturally, also deserves fond acknowledgment.

Note that the words "convict," "prisoner," and "inmate," "guard" and "officer," all meaning different things to different people, are used interchangeably and do not connote disrespect in any manner.

Jolene Babyak, 1996

Library of Congress Catalog Card Number: 88-70100
ISBN 0-9618752-0-8
Cover design by David Bullen
Cover photo and backcover photos courtesy of
  Philip F. Dollison and Corinne Dollison Edwards
Printed in the USA

Other Books by Jolene Babyak
Bird Man, The Many Faces of Robert Stroud

ARIEL VAMP PRESS
P.O. Box 3496
Berkeley, CA 94703

. . . dedicated to Art, Larry,
  and especially to Evelyn.

Contents

An armed Alcatraz officer stands on the deck of Tower #2, the Road tower, overlooking the Industries area and the yard wall. Little Alcatraz, a small rock visible in low tide, is left of the Industries building. (COURTESY OF PHIL DOLLISON)

At Last

On December 16, 1962, four months before the U.S. Penitentiary on Alcatraz Island closed, two prisoners finished cutting through the basement windows bars using saw blades. "I went up to the armory and checked out a rifle," said Officer Fred Freeman:

[Officer] Pickens and I went out the catwalk to industries and when we got to about #3 Tower, we spotted Parker. He was on what we call Little Alcatraz, [a small rock off the island]. He hurt his ankle and we kept him pinned down until the boat could pick him up. Every time he'd move, we'd fire a round off . . . just to keep him on that rock.

Richard Waszak, who had been an officer on Alcatraz since late 1959, remembers assigning two men:

They had their firearms and I posted [them] on top of Industries. . . . I started to head back and one of them started to shoot. They were firing at Little Alcatraz just to get Parker to stay on the rock.

"Boy!" said Mike Pitzer, a teenager at the time. "That was the first time I'd been around a prison break where they did any shooting." His father, Edmund Pitzer, had been transferred to Alcatraz only six months earlier, in June, 1962. This was their second Alcatraz escape attempt in that time. Mike, his parents and teenage sister, Doreen, were eating dinner in their island apartment when the escape siren sounded:

I went outside and [saw officers] up on the roof, and they were firing all kinds of shots. I thought they would blow the rock away! They even had two Coast Guard boats on the back side and [the prisoners] wouldn't give up. Then I remember the front guy holding him with a grappling hook and pulling him in.

Dick and Maryanne Waszak had been living on Alcatraz for three years. They had three children, ages two through seven, the last one born while they were on the island. Maryanne, a petite, vivacious woman, who was scared of living on Alcatraz the first few weeks, remembered that siren very well:

Everybody on the island knew you were supposed to bolt your doors, stay in, so the kids were in the house and the doors were locked. We had three doors to the hall [of the apartment building]. And the dining room door was just a flimsy, hollow-core door that wouldn't keep anybody out. We had a huge bookcase—filled—and it was heavy. I don't think anybody had ever moved it. 'Course, he took off and he says, 'Lock the doors.' Well, I did, but that door in the dining room's not going to keep anybody out. And there's that huge bookcase and I pushed it in front of the door, and I was a skinny, scrawny little gal at the time. But I got that in front of the door.

"I know exactly what I was wearing that day," her husband, Dick said. Although this was his first federal prison assignment, the short, enthusiastic Nebraska man remained in the federal prison service more than twenty years, retiring as an associate warden:

It was on a Sunday when Scott and Parker went. I had my trousers on and a white undershirt. I'd already taken my shirt off. And when the alarm went, I reported that way. I remember because [later] I was on the boat—we were out searching the waters—and it was so ungodly cold out there! And, of course, raining. And that's all I had on.

So went the last escape attempt from Alcatraz. Prisoners John Paul Scott and Darl Dee Parker were discovered missing from the kitchen crew at 5:40 PM on a drizzly, foggy Sunday—only minutes after the last prison count. The Scott–Parker attempt was the second escape incident that year. Although the decision to close Alcatraz had come as early as

---

Alcatraz:
The most famous federal prison in American history—yet one of the smallest. It held less than three hundred men at a time, or about one percent of all federal prisoners.

1961—a decision fortified by the more famous Morris-Anglin escape attempt in June of '62—the wheels of bureaucracy had turned slowly. But now, with this second escape attempt that year, the island prison would shut down within three months. It had been a calamitous year for those who lived and worked on Alcatraz. The notorious federal prison that had existed only twenty–nine years would finally close in March, 1963.

Alcatraz was home to about seventy-five kids that year, and I was one of them. Surprisingly, about sixty families and ten or so bachelors had always resided on "The Rock." Our fathers were the guards, maintenance men, lighthouse keepers, culinary officers, industries officials and administrators who worked "up top." Most of us crossed the San Francisco Bay five times a week to go to school in San Francisco. We played football and softball on the concrete parade ground that was our playground. We brought friends to Alcatraz and dazzled them with our prison stories.

At the top of our neighborhood was a maximum security penitentiary. Yet, I saw

The incredible escape route of John Paul Scott and Darl Dee Parker on December 16, 1962, took them from the basement up to the prison's roof, down the other side and behind one of the island's apartment buildings before they waded into the bay. Parker was found within minutes clinging to a small rock near the island. Scott washed up along the San Francisco shore a few hours later, dazed but alive. Warden Olin G. Blackwell commented that had Scott not washed up, he would have headed towards Hawaii "without benefit of a boat."

(NATIONAL MARITIME MUSEUM)

prisoners only from a distance and paid little attention to them. Our parents frequently said they felt safer living on Alcatraz than in San Francisco. There was no traffic, no burglaries; few of us, in fact, worried about security. It was a low–crime neighborhood, after all. Fences and locked gates were everywhere, yet some residents didn't locked their doors. Parents were far more concerned one of us might trip into the bay and float away.

There were provocative contrasts. Set so close to the city, Alcatraz was infamous and mysterious. Merely the name evoked strong emotional images and tiresome stereotypes. Because of movies, people imagined the worst about living there. They were incredulous: "Do you eat with the prisoners?" someone asked me once. "Aren't you scared?" No, I didn't, and I wasn't.

The film, *Birdman of Alcatraz,* was released while I lived on "The Rock," and much of what people knew about the prison came from that sentimental film. Robert Stroud, the "Bird Man," was not the patient scientist portrayed by actor Burt Lancaster. Instead, he was an eccentric, raw, avowed pederast who had murdered two men, and had also raised canaries in his cell at another prison. He was really the "Bird Man of Leavenworth." People vilify criminals, yet sympathize with them when they become prisoners—*or actors.* The public outcry became even more pronounced when a man reached "The Rock."

Other ironies existed there as well. Alcatraz was perhaps the most beautiful home I've ever had. On a breezy, crystal-clear day, the bay is a magical setting, with two bridges—one, the Golden Gate, perhaps the most famous bridge in the world—defining the perimeters of the dramatic skyline of San Francisco. The bay itself was breathtaking theatre. Ships slid under the Golden Gate past our island; pugged-nosed tug boats churned up the white caps. The waves were frequently dotted with boats and their glistening white, yawning sails. Yet, there stood Alcatraz, a mile-and-a-quarter out in the bay, a battleship-shaped rock mounted with a three-story, institutional-yellow prison. A flat island mountain lined with barbed wire and guard towers.

It was a peaceful setting, despite all, and perhaps the supreme irony of Alcatraz. In the last days before it finally closed, those of us who weren't prisoners on Alcatraz knew that we'd miss our "poor man's Hawaii."

We'd miss our 360 degree view of the Bay Area, we'd miss the fog horns that rattled our windows, the island Christmas parties, the summer watermelon feasts on the dock. We'd miss the boat that was always too early or too late to catch a movie in the city. We'd miss the excitement when the escape siren sounded.

The big house at the top of our neighborhood was a maximum security penitentiary with cells three tiers high. (PHIL DOLLISON)

Ironies and contrasts were a part of the setting. Only a mile-and-a-quarter from San Francisco—one of the most beautiful cities in the world—"The Rock" was a flat island mountain lined with barbed wire and guard towers. Here, the Golden Gate Bridge is seen through prison fences.

(NATIONAL MARITIME MUSEUM)

"Before the last of us left we took a boat ride around the island," Maryanne Waszak remembered. "We got all the kids, we sat on the front of the boat and I cried and he was crying—the whole bunch of us. It was sad to leave. We were all so close."

That was the feeling everyone shared. Although there had always been scandals, rumors, and even some backbiting among the employees and their families forced to live so close to work, a genuine feeling existed that we were all one family. "If you needed help," said LuAnne Freeman, "it was there."

At the end, even we were curious about the cell house, which most of the women and children had never seen. "I will never forget right after the last prisoners walked out," said Mike Pitzer:

I went in the cell block. My dad came up and we got to talking. 'Here's your chance to see what it's like in one of these cells.' And I went in one. There were no personal items in there but everything else was intact. And he slammed the door and left me! It blew my mind! I will never forget as long as I live. . . . The doors closed and they went clank—and there's a real hollow sound.

A prison officer opens a cell using gears located in a locked box at the end of each cell block. (PHIL DOLLISON)

The teenager entered the five-by-nine-foot cell his father opened for him and, like a prisoner, he couldn't see how the cell doors were activated. Gears were located on either side of the cell block and could be maneuvered to close one or all cell fronts. The levers resembled ones used on the famed San Francisco cable cars. And in some ways, the sound of a closing cell door is like the sound of a cable car on tracks. But such pleasantries don't remain. What occurs is a drum roll of heavy metal thundering across metal and concrete, as the door slides into position with a final metal-to-metal collision that echoes throughout the concrete building:

I thought, my God! For the first minute or two, it was like a game, but then I started yelling and I was ready to get out. And there was no answer. I walked up and grabbed hold of the bars thinking I could pull the door open. And I couldn't. All you could see was the cell across, and nobody and nothing! . . . That really hit me hard. I got kind of weak.

As famous then as it is today, Alcatraz was a curiosity to visitors who often could get no closer than a dime telescope along Fisherman's Wharf.
(PHOTO BY ROBERT J. HART; COURTESY OF JOHN BRUNNER)

Security was so strict when the first prisoners arrived in 1934 that train cars were transported by barge rather than be unloaded on the mainland. Building 64 at the dock, built by the U.S. Army as a barracks in 1904-06, stands on top of a Civil War-era fort, one of the original buildings on "The Rock." (NATIONAL MARITIME MUSEUM)

Moving On

Many times I'd hit the gangplank at a dead run. If the tide was high, it tilted only slightly down to the floating platform where the boat was moored.

But if the tide was out, as it was twice a day, that narrow, pulley-operated, tar-papered gangplank hung vertically, and your weight alone dropped it to the float. Breathless from my run after hearing the boat's whistle, I'd jump down the gangplank, balance on the rolling, heaving float and step across the plumbless deluge onto a pitching and yawing boat.

On nice days I sat outside—ducking the occasional crest of spray at the bow or watching the propellers churn and tickle the sea at the aft. But mostly, I sat inside. Alcatraz was only twelve minutes from San Francisco by boat, but the weather could change from a bright, clear city day to a gray, cold, foggy Alcatraz, and seem like a different month. I usually headed for the cargo hold where my friends were already seated. In 1962, I was a teenager and carrying on a hundred–year–old Alcatraz tradition. School was out and I was going home to Alcatraz.

Since the 1860s people had been crossing the bay bound for the prison island—first, the military families who occupied the island until 1933, then the federal prison families, who were part of the staff during the federal prison years.

Warden James A. Johnston and his family were among the first federal families to occupy the island. Johnston had been given the rare opportunity to oversee the remodeling of the old military prison on Alcatraz into the nation's most maximum security federal prison.

A sixty–year–old man in the prime of his life, Johnston's polish and quiet authority showed. From an Irish family with thirteen children, Johnston had been educated in

San Francisco and admitted to the California Bar Association in 1919.

A respected criminologist, lawyer, banker, public speaker and writer, Johnston's prison career began as early as 1912, when he became warden of California's vicious Folsom Prison. A decided progressive, he was said to have abolished corporal punishment, installed a ventilation system in the cell house, and begun a trusty farm outside the walls. In 1913, he became warden of San Quentin, California's maximum state prison with its extensive death row and gas chamber. Again, he was progressive. Remaining until 1925, he abolished stripes on prison clothing, established honor camps, a classification system and introduced religion. "If we take hate-filled, mentally warped men into prisons and do not earnestly endeavor to correct their wrong notions and replace their antisocial tendencies with finer, saner, and better ideas of their social obligations," he wrote in 1924, a year before becoming a San Francisco banker, "they may leave prison worse than when they entered, [and] the prison would be a menace to society."

But times had changed and so had Johnston. It was the Great Depression, the "dirty 30s," a time of massive unemployment, crime sprees and well-publicized prison escapes. The government needed an "escape-proof" prison to hold the nation's worst federal prisoners and they didn't want a progressive at the helm.

Warden Johnston didn't disappoint them. Alcatraz was designed to be the noose over the head of every federal prisoner. No one would be sentenced directly from the courts (although a few were), but would work his way there by behavioral problems in other prisons. There would be no parole directly from Alcatraz either. When a man transferred to "The Rock," he lost much of his "good time," time off his sentence for good behavior, and had to earn it back before a transfer out. It would be transfer or "toes up," said an infamous early prisoner, "Blackie" Audett, later.

Johnston fortified the island's security. He installed tool-proof cell fronts to B and C blocks, he added towers and barbed wire, new gun galleries inside the cell house, tear gas canisters in the dining room, metal detectors at the dock and near the Industries, so prisoners could be checked often for contraband. He decided that one guard would serve for every three prisoners (ten or thirteen to one was normal). There would be no commissary, no radio, no newspapers, no honor system, no trusties. Prisoners would receive one visit per month for about an hour–and–a–half, visits conducted through glass and a telephone.

Alcatraz was a prison for a hundred–and–two years— from 1860 until 1933 as an Army penitentiary and from 1934 until 1963 as a federal prison.

From the beginning the government intentionally projected an image of Alcatraz as *the* escape-proof prison. This widely-reprinted photo, with Attorney General Homer Cummings, left, and Warden James A. Johnston inspecting the Alcatraz officer corps, attempted to show the government's determination to deal harshly with depression-era criminals and helped set the "escape-proof" myth in motion. Initially, officers were handpicked from prisons around the nation; later it was often difficult to get men to transfer to "The Rock." (NATIONAL MARITIME MUSEUM)

A Texas newspaper follows the trail of a train carrying Chicago gangster Al Capone (below), and others from Atlanta penitentiary bound for Alcatraz. Famous prisoners like Capone and the media attention during the "Great Depression" accounted for the instant notoriety of Alcatraz. (TOP PHOTO COURTESY OF THE DEL RIO EVENING NEWS.)

But what signaled Johnston's turnaround was his establishment of the dreaded "silent system," a throwback to an era when prisoners were forbidden to converse. The silence would be deafening. And cruel. And increasingly difficult to enforce. Within four years, the rule was abandoned and never again brought back.

By the time two trains of prisoners from Atlanta and Leavenworth penitentiaries rolled halfway across the country bound for Alcatraz, the island prison was already infamous. Yet, the ironies were also apparent. Barbara Johnston Ford, the warden's youngest daughter, was happily unaware of the hoopla. She recalls hearing "rumors" that prisoners would arrive by train in August and September, 1934.

"Then in August," Esther Faulk, wife of Isaac Faulk and one of the first families, remembered, "the first prisoners arrived, among them Al Capone." She laughed. "And women and children were requested to stay indoors while the prisoners were locked in their cells. ...Well, we kind'a snuck a look before the boat docked."

Infamous escape artist and train robber Roy Gardner was on one of the trains, as were "Machine Gun" Kelly, Harvey Bailey, Charlie Berta, "Blackie" Audett and about two hundred others. But newspapers were mostly concerned about the train they called the "Al Capone Special." The "Chicago Czar" was aboard.

Capone, also known as "Scarface," was the most notorious gangland mobster in the 20th Century. Implicated in scores of murders, reputed leader of the Italian Mafia, a strong family man, a pimp and a bootlegger, Capone ran Chicago with machine guns. He was finally imprisoned on an eleven–year federal income tax evasion charge, serving seven. By 1934, when he arrived on Alcatraz to serve four-and-a-half years there, his life was going downhill. Untreated syphilis had begun to erode his brain. Docile and at times confused, he finally departed Alcatraz in 1939 and died at home in 1947, at age forty–eight.

The day he arrived on the train with the other convicts, kids on Alcatraz squatted behind the balcony railings of 64 building, vying to see if they could spot the great Capone. Caroline Weinhold Hoffman, fifteen at the time, and whose father, Henry Weinhold, would one day be captain of the guards, was one of the kids watching the arrival on the dock below.

Josephine Michelson, wife of an Alcatraz officer, looked out her window. "Our apartment was right up over the dock. ...I watched the first trainload of prisoners come over from the mainland. They just unhooked the whole train, pushed the cars onto a big [barge] and barged them over."

Fourteen–year–old Alfred Klineschmidt vividly remembers the unshaven cons with "leg irons and chains running between their legs."

Those early Alcatraz kids didn't miss the significance of the event, and the camaraderie of being in the center of some larger purpose. Alcatraz had been given a mandate and the parade of convicts had begun.

Islanders quickly saw advantages to their lives on Alcatraz. Children were safely tucked away from busy streets, in a village where everyone knew everyone else. The view was breathtaking and particularly momentous at this time because both the Golden Gate and the Bay bridges were under construction.

Children were fascinated and often influenced by the bay. Said Klineschmidt, who later became a career officer in the Navy Reserves, "I could tell every boat that went out the harbor by the whistle. I made it a hobby. I'd write it down, put the pitch on it and stuff—the *S.S. Yale*, the *Ruth Alexander,* the *Mariposa,* the *Lurline*, the *Matson*—I could tell when they were going to sail."

Although the residents were reluctant to admit it, they also shared in the notoriety of their neighbors. "Al Capone used to deliver our milk," one well-meaning women said flatly. She was mistaken, but everyone felt some connection. "Mrs. Capone used to ride the boat with us," said George Steere. "His wife. She was a blond and dressed fit to kill, and she always had a chauffeur and body guards with her, but they couldn't get on the boat. She sat by herself all the time."

Capone's mother was said to have arrived once and when going through the metal detector, had set off the alarm so many times an officer's wife was asked to search her clothing. Talk among islanders about prisoners' visitors was never malicious, but it was greased by a sense of amused superiority. And stories involving famous cons were fair game for exaggeration. Mrs. Capone, who barely spoke English, was visibly embarrassed at having to strip down to her corset, revealing the metal stays that had

Lieutenant Isaac Faulk, his wife Esther, and their children Herbert, Edward and Ruth outside their Alcatraz cottage. They lived on the island for nineteen years. (ESTHER FAULK)

13

tripped the metal detector.

As more families arrived, the old military Officer's Club became the scene of more activities—dinners, Halloween and Christmas parties. There was a two-lane bowling alley in the basement, ping pong and pool tables. Teenagers held dances and invited their lucky friends from San Francisco.

But the island prison wasn't the most ideal place to live. It was shaped like a battleship and laid out on three levels. Up top were the prison, the warden's mansion and the light house keepers' residence. The rest of us lived on the second level. Below us were the rocky beaches and the icy cold currents of the San Francisco Bay.

The old military base that had preceded us had been in almost continuous construction since the 1850s, with structures built on top of others—such as 64 building, the imposing former barracks which straddled the dock and the second level of the island, and served as our apartment building. It had been built on top of an old fort.

The old Army parade ground, a two–acre concrete slab, was our playground and village "common." Apartment buildings A, B, and C, a duplex occupied by the captain's and associate warden's families, four cottages, a tiny recreation hall and playground equipment were on the perimeter. What tiny patches of grass that existed on Alcatraz were forbidden to us kids. And although the island was lush with ivy, ice plant, blueberry bushes, geraniums, honeysuckle, wild poppies, huge Agave plants and eucalyptus trees, most of these were located in restricted areas. Thus, the concrete was our batting field, skating rink, tennis court and touch football gridiron. Just walking across that parade ground was a bone-chilling experience. Although surrounded by buildings, it was a concrete prairie on which the winds whipped furiously. If the fog were thick, we could walk across it without seeing a single building. At night the lights were often shrouded in a thick, pea-soup fog, illuminated by the lighthouse beam as it faded through every five seconds.

About five hundred people—prisoners and staff families—lived mostly peacefully on a twenty–two–acre island.

Alcatraz *wasn't* safe, but surprisingly, it wasn't the prisoners our parents worried about. It was the cliffs and the swift bay tides that could sweep you out to sea; it was the little bridges into the apartments at 64 building, which were three stories above a concrete alley, known since the Army days as "Chinatown." It was the rocky boat rides and the mischievous sea. It was the needle-sharp Agave plants that clung to the cliffs and bring about serious injury if anyone had fallen on them. It was that old concrete playground. The parents worried, but we didn't care.

Alcatraz was a battleship-shaped island laid out in three tiers. Around this two-acre slab of concrete were the residents' living quarters: 64 building rising from the dock at right, the four cottages, the associate warden's/captain's duplex, center bottom, (my home for a year), apartment buildings A, B, and C, left, and an officers' recreation hall in the center of the parade ground. Up top is the lighthouse and residence, the warden's house, the medical assistant's quarters, and the prison building.

(ARTHUR M. DOLLISON)

"We were hot-shot roller skaters," remembers Joyce Rose Ritz, whose dad was commissary officer and helped inmate details paint many of the warning signs on the island. "We used to put up a pole and a [sheet] and the wind would catch, and you'd zip across [the parade ground] thirty miles an hour. About all the kids broke their bones at one time or another," she said:

We used to climb the rocks around the [prison] workshops, which was fairly dangerous, I'm sure. As strict as Warden Johnston was, he was busy putting the prison together, and he wasn't really dealing with the youngsters yet. After the place settled down they realized what we could get into [and] the rules were set down.

That group of youngsters—about fifty in all—had more run of the island than any group thereafter, because later more fences separated the prison from us. George Steere lived next to the cellhouse, so kids played up at his house. Klineschmidt remembers playing football just outside the prison, and on Sundays sneaking up to the building to listen to the convict band.

The danger was there. Prisoners worked in our areas and some we saw almost everyday. But they were never without a guard and they were forbidden to talk to us or approach us. There were stories of prisoners tossing a ball to a kid, or tipping their hats in greeting. Bill Dolby, a nine-year-old when he moved on with his family in 1944, said he was "sort of" introduced to some of the more friendly dock inmates by the more experienced kids. "There was one they called 'Mickey Mouse,' one 'Popeye,' and there was a 'Donald Duck' too," he said. "We'd talk to 'em, yell at 'em:

One of our major recreations was playing handball and the best thing was a tennis ball that had the fuzz taken off. There were two ways to take the fuzz off. One was to rub it on concrete and the other was to throw it down to the guys on the dock and they'd take it into the shop and buzz it off with a wire power brush. They'd do that for us. They seemed like average people, they weren't monsters or anything. I can remember asking my dad, 'What did this guy do? What did that guy do?' That kind of diffused any sympathy.

My first mixed recollections of Alcatraz at age seven were the smell of the beautiful, orange starfish that I dried on my windowsill, and at night, the pitch and yaw of convicts on a vocal rampage. (They'd yell at times and drag their cups on the bars. Officer Bill Long later said they would often stage a welcoming party whenever new prisoners came on the island.) I remember asking about the noise as I was tucked into bed, and being reassured that it was just inmates, as we called them, letting off steam. Although my parents didn't communicate fear to me, or even hatred of prisoners, I knew to keep my distance, and that behavior generated a childlike feeling of awe and a hushed reverence, as if prisoners were special people. Special, but dangerous perhaps. I found them fascinating—but I kept my distance.

Standing on the windy parade ground in front of 64 building, are (r. to l.) my mother, Evelyn O'Brien Dollison, my sister, Corinne Dollison Edwards and me. Life moved normally among the staff families on Alcatraz. This photo was taken on a Sunday, just after church services. (PHOTO BY PHIL DOLLISON; COURTESY OF CORINNE EDWARDS)

My father, Arthur M. Dollison, was transferred to Alcatraz in 1953, as office manager of the prison Industries. Although he had been in the federal prison service for fifteen years, he knew little about Alcatraz. Everyone knew about the city's top tourist attraction, he said later, "But no one knew where to catch the boat:

The people at the hotel didn't know. They told me which bus to take, but the driver didn't know either. He turned in his seat and called out, 'Anybody know where to catch the boat to Alcatraz?' No one answered, but several looked me over carefully and I shrank a little. I could guess what they were thinking. It wouldn't enter their minds that I could be reporting for work. And since I wasn't an escapee, there was only one possibility: my brother, or son or father was a prisoner. They weren't sure whether to feel sorry for me, or be scared, and that gave us something in common, because I had mixed feelings about my connection to Alcatraz, and fright and sorrow came out just about even.

Dollison finally found the cityside dock, and although he was recognized by the Alcatraz boat officer—a man with whom he had worked before—the officer called the Alcatraz Control Center before letting him board.

My family arrived in the spring of 1954, and took up residence in the dismal 64 building. The building itself was like a set from a theatrical play about tenement life in New York City. But the rent was cheap, and the view was spectacular—particularly if you were coming from a drab prison town in the Midwest.

We'd see prisoners working nearby, separated from us by a fence. Once, when I was eight, a prisoner found a hard rubber ball in the weeds and beckoned to me. I shyly approached, as the guard stood there, and the man pushed the ball through the fence to me. It was a proud moment; I had in my hand *the* most valued item on Alcatraz— the coveted black handball that had rolled down the hill from over the prison yard wall. And it had been given to my by a prisoner. It was my first "real life" conflict—whether to say thank you to an adult, or to not speak to a convict. I'm equally sure it was my first compromise. I may have said thanks, but he probably didn't hear it.

Prisoners had nick names that we heard around the kitchen table, names with stories attached to them, such as the man known as the "Green Lizard," who was rumored to

The Alcatraz commemorative postal stamp from the U.S. Post Office in 64 building. Some prisoners' families felt embarrassed when getting letters post-marked "Alcatraz." Staff members and families, on the other hand, were proud of the stamp.   (JEAN LONG)

ALCATRAZ
IS SPANISH
FOR PELICAN

ALCATRAZ ISLAND, CALIF.

have eaten lizards on a dare, or one called "Suitcase Sally," who, during World War
II, allegedly smuggled lead in suitcases, or "Bumpy," or "Porkchops," who was fond
of eating them, or "Dog," or "Stubby," or "Creepy," or "Jack Rabbit," who "ran like
a rabbit" in an escape attempt once. Although the names were amusing, these men
often had long, compounded sentences aggravated by incidents in other prisons.
Alcatraz was, after all, the end of the line.

Some officers kept notebooks to help them identify prisoners, and no doubt, on a
sleepless night, a man might become obsessive about those notes. "Murder-rape-
escape," or "forty–two years, killing," might make an officer wonder why he had
brought his family to this. "Life–plus–year–plus–day—murder, rape, escape," might
explain why one man went off the deep end, and "good barber," next to a man's name
might explain why he got out of "the hole" a little sooner.

Notes like "Death-life-treason," or "ring leader of North Carolina escape," would
trail a man from one prison to another. "Electrician and good. Also expert lock-
picker," went another warning.

"He was a self-mutilator," one officer told me, peering into his notebook and
reading, "Five years, life—murder, will screw anything that will slow down."

Alcatraz housed *federal* prisoners—men convicted of bank robbery, kidnapping,
crossing state lines to avoid arrest, postal robbery, income tax evasion, draft dodg-
ing—charges that don't seem as significant as murder or rape, which are more often
state crimes. But the Alcatraz population represented only *one per cen*t of the federal
prison population in the nation, and they were often violent offenders. One man served
a concurrent six years and life for robbery and murder of a custodial officer: while a
prisoner held the officer he slashed him repeatedly with a knife and beat him with a
chair. Another was already serving a fifteen–five–year murder sentence when he
killed an Alcatraz prisoner. And he threatened to kill someone else who had spit on
him. Another, Jimmy Grove, had sixty–some disciplinary reports at Atlanta,
Leavenworth and Alcatraz, at least nineteen of which were serious charges—stab-
bings, murder, attempts to strangle, self–mutilation.

Another, a famous Puerto Rican national, was serving eight–one years for wildly
shooting in the U.S. Congress. Another was serving life for presiding over a prisoner-
of-war camp in which American servicemen were tortured. Of another, serving life
plus twenty–one years for murder, an official wrote, "could let two white men and one

Negro out of [D block] if he transferred." (Some prisoners willingly went to segregation for their own protection.)

Most were disadvantaged kids and had begun with minor teenage delinquency charges which they compounded with escapes and assaults, until at a young age, they were already in maximum security institutions. Yet, many had been violent all their lives. One convict serving five years for auto theft admitted in court having murdered his foster mother when he was thirteen years old. Another serving twenty years for bank robbery and manslaughter had driven a pick into a man's head.

Olin G. Blackwell, who was the last warden on Alcatraz, said once about a prisoner there. "He explained to me how he killed [a prisoner in another prison]:

He had this piece of brick in a sock and [the guy] was laying on his cot asleep and he rammed him down across the head and he said, 'That blood flew all over the walls and everything.' And he said, 'You shot a hog, haven't you, Mr. Blackwell?' And I said, 'Yes,' He said, 'You know how they stick their legs out and kick?' And I said, 'Yeah.' He said, 'That's just the way he did.' Well now, is that a man you send to Alcatraz?

Officers inspect laundry for contraband in the foreground while prisoners load laundry and cargo nets into the freight bin. Although all fresh water had to be barged to the island at great expense, the prison had one of the largest laundries in the federal prison system. (PHIL DOLLISON)

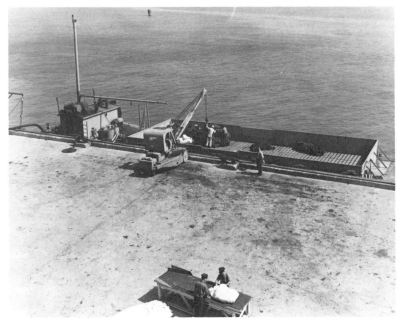

The danger was there. Everyone knew, as officer George Gregory once said, "All you have to do is take the bone out of a T-bone steak and you've got an excellent weapon." It just never came down the hill. And our fathers didn't dwell on it.

The inconvenience of Alcatraz concerned us more. In those early days, the boat made only about nine round trips a day to the city.

But Esther Faulk had a baby when she lived on Alcatraz, the same year eight other women there had babies, she said. And she and her family stayed nineteen years. Marvin and Winifred Orr stayed twenty–one. The Bergens remained sixteen. They could have moved to San Francisco, but they didn't want to.

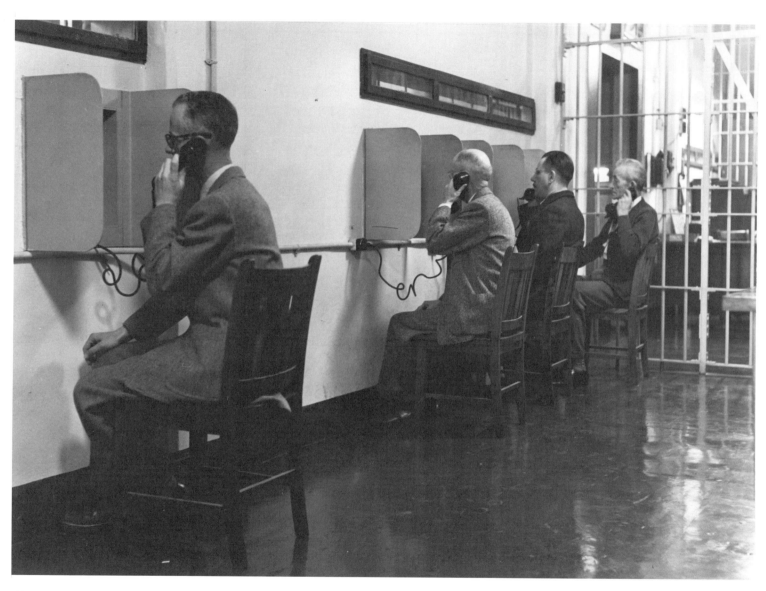

Alcatraz administrators pose as visitors talking through telephones to convicts in this early photograph. Few prisoners received visitors and rarely would four be seated simultaneously. Most prisoners were from the Midwest or the east and few families would travel such a great distance for one visit a month for under two hours. Throughout the years this restriction was not relaxed. (PHIL DOLLISON)

Tower watch was a long, tedious vigil—an officer stood an eight hour shift for a minimum tour of three months, sometimes six months. Here the Road tower (also known as Two tower)—manned twenty–four hours a day—is silhouetted against the faded backdrop of the San Francisco skyline. Towers were often staffed by new officers, or men who had trouble working closely with prisoners. (NAT'L MARITIME MUS.)

The Assignment

One tower was a coal black, octagonal cell with shatterproof glass. Three stories tall, it sat atop four spider legs and a spiral staircase which ended at a locked hatch in the deck. Of the six towers it was the principal post, located on the dock and staffed twenty–four hours a day.

"They shoved you in the dock tower on the morning watch for eight hours and boy that was rough!" said Irving (Levy) Levinson, a small man with a wry sense of humor. "No one to talk to, you don't see a damn thing. And you got to keep your eyes open for the lieutenant!"

Levinson was shot at once during his tower watch.

From here the officer saw the length of the dock, the family quarters in 64 Building, the north cell house wall, the yard wall and Kitchen cage, and beyond to the water tank and Hill tower. He could not see the Industries area, or the Road tower blocked by the prison directly south of him.

The Road, or Two tower, was the second most important peripheral post, and also manned twenty–four hours a day. Here the San Francisco skyline was to the officer's back. He faced the southeast side of the prison, the yard, its posts, and the yard wall gate through which, during weekdays, a convoy of prisoners walked down the stairs to the Industries area. At lunch, and again at about 4:00 PM, he watched them stroll back to the cell house. He saw the warden's house, the medical technical assistant's house and the lighthouse to the east. He couldn't see the Dock tower.

The Main tower, another twenty–four hour post, sat squat atop the cell house. The Power House tower, the Hill tower and the Model Roof tower were manned only during daylight hours and mostly protected the Industries area when convicts were out of their cells.

Two "cages," the Kitchen cage, located just behind the cell house, manned when the culinary prisoners were out of their cells, and the Dining Room cage, staffed by the Hill

The Hill tower, left center, was attached to the prison building and the Model Roof tower, right, by a long catwalk. Both were staffed during the day when prisoners were out of their cells. At mealtimes, the armed Hill tower guard walked the catwalk to the Dining Room cage, which ran the length of the dining room outside the building, and patrolled while prisoners ate inside the dining room. The building left of the smokestack is the power house, where an old diesel-powered generator pumped direct current electricity around the island. The island's electrical system, designed by the Army, became more decrepit as time passed. (PHOTOGRAPH BY ROBERT J. HART; COURTESY OF JOHN BRUNNER)

tower man while prisoners ate, and the yard wall posts, completed the peripheral security.

Towers were usually three-month rotated tours which could be repeated. They were usually reserved for new officers, sometimes used as punishment, or relegated to those who because of physical or emotional factors couldn't work the cell house. Most prison guards, especially new men, pulled tower duty at least once. Almost all hated it.

As the custodial superstructure, towers were well-fortified:

Former officer Kenneth Bush stands on the 64 building balcony with the Dock tower in the background. One of the tallest, freestanding towers ever built, it replaced an earlier less well fortified tower built during the U.S. Army prison days. (COURTESY OF CORINNE EDWARDS)

The guard in the yard wall had a Thompson submachine gun and a .45 calibre pistol [said former Alcatraz captain Phil Bergen]. All other towers, in addition to those, had a shotgun and a 30.06 Springfield. So they had a shotgun, pistol, rifle and Thompson submachine gun. They also had a gas cartridge gun which could fire both short and long-range gas cartridges.

Except for a wayward blast from a ship's horn as it skulked into the bay, little distracted the tower officer as he saw past his reflection to the panorama outside. The sun set and the city lights began to twinkle. At night, the Alcatraz lighthouse beam penetrated the darkness with stunning regularity. On clear, moonlit nights, a distant, deep, uneven shadow moved like a front on the water and foretold the freshening of the breezes. Watch officers hiked up their collars, hunched their shoulders and saw the coruscating beauty in the cold and silence.

The Dock tower officers' most important job was the boat watch. He kept the key. Every time the boat was ready to be boarded, he clipped its engine key to a wire that stretched from the tower railing down to the dock, and cranked it down to the dock lieutenant.

Each time the boat returned to the island, the boat

officer tied the lines, attached the key to the wire, and cranked it back to the tower, then helped the passengers off. The tower day shift saw lots of dock activity; the night shift saw almost none. If this were a normal night, the last boat at midnight and the key exchange would be the most activity One tower saw on his entire shift.

"Towers there were very monotonous," said Bill Long, a tall, broad-shouldered, expressive man whom the cons called "Big Stoop." "You just sat and looked until your eyeballs hurt."

When the weather was miserable the post was miserable. The fog settled and the foghorns droned, while the watch officers listened for any movement in the gray jungle. Towers had no heat. One man said later that the coldest he'd ever been was one summer when he pulled tower duty on Alcatraz.

The island patrol officer, on the other hand, kept watch by walking the island. His job at night was also repetitive and dreary.

Using his flashlight sparingly, he began his rounds along the beach at the lower east end of the island. If it were a normal night, this was a tedious, silent, nagging cold vigil. Even on the leeward side of Alcatraz, the damp seeped through the woolen overcoats and dark, double-breasted suits with a vengeance. The patrolman's job was to surprise anyone or anything that trespassed.

"If you ever thought about spooks," said Long, "that was the time to do it." This job also fell to new officers, but they soon learned to distinguish between suspicious sounds and those of surf and seagulls. On more than one occasion, though, an officer skirmished with a yelping sea lion lolling up on the beach, or panicked upon stumbling over a thick, decomposed shark someone had hauled in and left to die.

"We had a real rat problem for awhile," said Phil Bergen. (It was something I hadn't known as a child.)

[In] low tide you could walk out into an area which under normal conditions would be under water. And there would be a lot of stuff down on the beach and all the rats would come down to eat it. … The rats didn't like to be interfered with and they were big, healthy, mean-looking so-and-sos. I felt that on more than one occasion I was driven off. When you see them in the dark, what you see are those evil little eyes reflected in your flashlight. It looked like a million of them. But of course it wasn't that. Several hundred probably.

Inside the cell house, the lid was as tightly screwed on as on the glass jars in which we kids used to trap bumblebees.

No carpeting, no wood, no fabrics softened the metal and cement kennel that was the officer's workplace and the prisoner's home. Nothing muffled the noise riveting off walls and shiny cement floors. Nor was the sharp disinfectant smell a comfort, nor the gray and green smoke-dulled paint a welcome sight. Nothing smoothed the hollow, draconian penalty of what was in the 1940s and '50s a maximum security penitentiary.

Entering the main corridor, called "Broadway," one–hundred–sixty–eight cells faced one another. The accumulative sight was awesome; a warehouse of cells three tiers high, stacked beneath skylights that emitted a dull, rheumy light. It looked unnatural. It looked like a human wasp's nest.

Three-hundred-thirty-six cells, in three detached blocks—B, C and D—made up the Alcatraz penal colony. (Block A was never retooled and was used mainly for overfill from segregation in D block or for inmate–court.)

For the convict, the day began at 6:30 AM Breakfast at 7:00. Works details were racked out at about 8:00 and returned at approximately 11:45 AM. After lunch, work details were again moved at 1:00, and returned at 4:00 PM. (On foggy days, those who worked on island details or in Industries were returned to their cells early, or in some cases, laid in their cells for security reasons.) Supper was scheduled at 4:30 PM. Lights out at 9:30. Those temporarily without job assignments were held all day in their cells. There was little recreation, no professional counseling, no ongoing groups, no classes, no television and until the mid–1950s, no radio in their cells.

Even among prison officers, boredom and frustration was a problem. During the day, cell house traffic to work, the dining room and yard kept officers busy. After each major movement a prison–wide count was taken and called onto the Control Center. Tower officers sometimes shifted positions (during mealtimes, for example, the Hill tower man patrolled outside the prison in a cage than ran the length of the dining room.) But there was little traffic during weekends, and virtually none at night. Bored officers had to manage bored prisoners. And to the degree *that* lid was screwed on, made for more tension among officers.

To add to the problem, Alcatraz was often short-staffed. It needed a hundred–and–ten men to operate effectively, but often got by with only a hundred. Of those, about twenty-five were on sick call, annual leave, or their day off, leaving about seventy–five men to run a prison with about two–hundred–sixty prisoners. Sometimes lieutenants had barely

One of the smallest federal prisons, Alcatraz generally held about two–hundred–eighty prisoners. Men didn't transfer here because of their crimes, but because of the behavior in other prisons. Most were classified as "escape–risk."

Only the gun gallery officers were armed, and they were locked in well–fortified positions. Officers on the floor were never armed. They were also forbidden to carry pocket knives or nail files. Keys were kept in the gun galleries, and it was against regulations for a floor officer to hold keys longer than necessary to use them. Despite the possibility of danger, few officers were ever attacked. (PHIL DOLLISON)

enough men to cover each position.

This sea of countervailing tension for both staff and inmates boiled and ebbed constantly. My father sat in a glass office when he was superintendent of Industries, an office in the middle of one of the shops with a full view of the surrounding activities. He didn't talk about his work, or about prisoners much, but he often spoke of the tension which rose and fell like the bay tides that lapped against the island.

He could become vaguely aware that a shop seemed suddenly quiet, or that the population in general was withdrawing, and then abruptly, a prisoner could poke his head in the doorway—as happened once—and state that there was a dead man in the laundry, "in case you're interested." Art Dollison looked up sharply. "At least I think he's dead," the prisoner said calmly.

The kind of man who worked at Alcatraz differed little from men in other federal penitentiaries. The older among them had hired on during the depression. The younger men broke in during the 1950s, at times when unemployment was high. As a group they differed little from those who entered the postal service, business, or the clergy.

But generally speaking, the older men, only twice removed from the pioneering stock of America, were perhaps a little more gruff, stern, and hard-nosed.

E. J. Miller was a classic example. Miller was one of the first associate wardens—in those days called deputy warden—under Warden Johnston. While Johnston was the upper–crust, well educated good–guy cop, Miller was the diamond in the rough playing the bad cop. On day-to-day matters, Miller was judge and jury.

A hot-tempered, pugnacious, thick-skinned, barrel-chested, old-time prison guard, Miller was, by most accounts, fair and well liked, and described by one kid as "friendly," and "nice." Nonetheless, he displayed characteristics the public perceived as

(COURTESY OF PHIL DOLLISON)

stereotypical—gruff, heartless and burly.

"The Dutchman," former prisoner Dale Stamphill called him, "screamed at the top of his voice and you'd think he was going crazy. But after it was over, that was the end of it. He didn't hold a grudge."

"Miller would come into the cell house and the inmates would boo him, just 'cause they liked 'im," said officer Marvin Orr, who laughed heartily at the memory. "They wanted to get him mad, see, so they could watch 'im:

One time when [my son] Bob was about eight years old, he picked up the phone and dialed the fire alarm by mistake. That thing went off and Miller picked up the phone, and he starts barking. And Bob drops the phone and runs! [Orr laughed.] That's how vicious his voice would sound.

"He was liked, and he was feared, and he was hated, all rolled in one," said former prisoner, Clarence Carnes. Cons called him "Jughead," and "Meathead," a typical derisive con name, and several men remembered an incident when Miller became furious because a new arrival accidentally called him "Mr. Meathead."

Miller was legendary for cussing out anyone who crossed him. But he related easily to prisoners. He liked making bets with them, using segregated "hole time" as the wager. Benjamin Rayborn, a former con who paroled out and became a law researcher for the San Diego Federal Defenders Project, said that Miller was a baseball nut:

If you said you thought the Dodgers would beat the Cardinals and won, you got out [of the hole]. He'd make another bet. 'I'm out now,' you'd say. 'That's all right, you'll be back! We'll count it on the next time.'

The kind of man who took the job and liked it was often a man who found interaction with prisoners to be fascinating. A dry, droll sense of humor helped. "Greatest stories in the world," said George Gregory, an Alcatraz federal employee for many years.

Gregory had been a U.S. Marine who had been injured during World War II. The federal prison service helped him throughout his yearlong recovery, then hired him on. In late 1946 he transferred to Alcatraz.

A bachelor on Alcatraz, he played the role to an amused female audience and a slightly concerned male audience. During the '50s he turned down promotions to other prisons because he liked the Bay Area, and eventually married and retired there. It may have hurt his career, however. He was a junior officer, and sometimes made "acting' lieutenant, skipping over other senior officers, who resented it. He sometimes remained acting lieutenant for months at a time, and groused that it was a good way to get a lieutenant's responsibilities on a junior officer's pay. "At least seventy percent of the persons who work in prisons shouldn't be there," he scoffed. "And they'd probably say the same about me."

But he found the people fascinating. "Convicts were pretty proud of their caps," he said remembering the blue-gray railroad caps they wore. "And one time a guy's hat gets drop-bombed by a sea gull. And another con says, 'Wait—I'll get some toilet paper.' After he leaves another convict says to the first guy, 'How dumb can *he* be? By the time he gets back with toilet paper, that sea gull'll be long gone!'

Ten Alcatraz officers pose in 1953. Over the years the guard's uniform resembled a policeman's uniform less and less (see page 11 for comparison), until, in the 1970s, a more casual look of blazers and slacks became common. Only two officers have been identified here; Captain Emil Rychner, bottom left, and Deane Dorsey, lower right. (COURTESY OF HAZEL DORSEY ANDERSON)

Gregory wasn't as hot-tempered as Miller, and by no means in the same category, yet he wasn't afraid to diffuse the sting of such a man with his biting humor. Warden Edwin B. Swope was another old-time prison man, like E.J. Miller, yet with a difference. Most prisoners, and many in the staff, actively disliked him. The second warden of Alcatraz, Swope reigned from 1948 until 1955. He was well known for riding roughshod over his officers, pitting one man against another, and plummeting morale in his wake. There were many amusing stories about him.

Several officers remembered that when he moved off the island in 1955, he assigned prisoners to move his belongings to the island truck for passage to the dock. Gregory was at the truck when one prisoner came out of the warden's house carrying his shotgun.

Swope had a dog, something I and every kid on the island remembered during those years. (Bureau regulations forbid dogs or cats on prison grounds.) Whenever Bureau officials came to the island, Swope dispatched a guard to hide the animal on the mainland for a while.

Swope regularly put his arm around whomever he was talking to—officers and prisoners alike—calling him "M'boy," in a friendly, condescending fashion that many disliked. He did it once to Gregory. The officer pulled Swope's arm off, then deliberately examined his hand until Swope asked him what was he looking at.

"I just wanted to see if there was a knife in it," Gregory responded.

An officer, left, checks the daily roster while inmates move to their assignments. "Convicts," George Gregory said, "had the greatest stories in the world." (PHIL DOLLISON)

The men who arrived later to become federal prison officers were of a different generation. They resembled the businessmen of the 1950s. They felt men like Miller and Swope were too hard-nosed and unenlightened. And they sometimes regarded their peers as little better. When asked casually what was the difference between prisoners and officers, former Alcatraz Medical Technical Assistant Tom Reeves remarked cynically, "There's more sociopaths among the prisoners."

Although it was a wry, comical remark, there's no denying the dynamics of prison of which he was hinting: a group of men guarding others. Within that framework lies an undercurrent of suspicion and emotional turmoil.

Alcatraz, like all prisons, contained a limited population with a lowered cultural level; While their intelligence level mirrored the general population, they averaged an eighth grade education. Some didn't test beyond third or fifth grade, or had learning disabilities. Many were emotionally disturbed—often severely. Most were poorly skilled. The group as a whole was unstable and incohesive, participation in criminal activity being the basic common characteristic. Short tempers and frustrations provoked quick anger that had a compounding effect on their situation. Convicts were transferred in and out for custodial reasons; friendships were limited.

Particularly at Alcatraz there was widespread ignorance of events, news, and time, keeping prisoners at a distance from the real world and fostering a demoralizing feeling that no one outside cared.

Fights, triangles, rumors and manipulations ebbed and flowed constantly at Alcatraz, often because of the extreme boredom. Prisoners could find themselves in scrapes that sometimes lost them their jobs, their friends, or their self-respect. They wrote long, conciliatory explanations to authorities. "Mr. Donaldson: Please excuse the liberty I take in writing you this letter but I was wondering if you were going to give me the back Pay for running the 2 mechines [sic] since April..." wrote one man to Industries Superintendent, Arthur Dollison. The tack was one of pleas, conciliation, bargaining and hope, the victim trying to obtain some bit of fairness. "I am sorry to write you a letter of this sort. Please believe..." wrote another prisoner about another incident.

"...Please believe: I am disgusted with myself for my part in the fracas and promise you I will make the greatest possible effort to negate a recurrent..." wrote a man to both the warden and the superintendent. Such letters often contained promises: "If I am guilty of any of the foregoing I am to consider my job to be a forfeit..."

Such unmasked, cloying humility seldom elicited the desired effect. Not when the most common type of communication from a guard was a command, and the most common refrain from a prisoner was a question. Moreover, the expressed humility was at odds with the sudden violence. A cauldron of felt and real injustices boiled, and prisoners had an excess of time to stew, scheme and connive. In such a situation, ridicule, smirking insolence, sarcasm, withering, domineering mockery and contempt were normal reactions among prisoners.

"Popularity was power in prison," said Clarence Carnes, a long-time prisoner on Alcatraz. "Other prisoners didn't touch you if you had friends."

Among guards, although few characteristics determine who becomes one, the sublimi- nal conditioning *after* a man takes the job is difficult to avoid, and is expressed in increasingly ironic and paradoxical ways. This is true in any maximum security peniten- tiary. In talking about Alcatraz officers' attitudes, one old-timer and former officer said, "They thought those [prisoners] were *animals* and most of them were." Everyone who had ever been in a max pen knew there was some truth to that, but few would say how much officers contributed to it by their own attitudes.

Some men were far more obvious about their feelings for the "degenerates," "homos," and other "undesirables" they guarded. "Some of them guards," said one Alcatraz officer, "didn't like niggers." It was one man's revealing statement.

And although most officers aren't prejudiced or antagonistic, interaction between officer and prisoner is at best a flawed one. To prisoners, guards are the enemy. Yet interaction between prisoners was far more dangerous.

Most assaults in any given year were prisoner-upon-prisoner. Thirty-three assaults occurred on Alcatraz in 1958, for example, as listed in a report to Washington. Of those, twenty–nine were inmate–on–inmate. Most were fist fights, but prisoners also used knives, a metal pipe, a trumpet, a chair, and an iron weight that year.

Phil Bergen, Captain of the Guards 1949–55. (PHIL DOLLISON)

"They were always ready," said Phil Bergen, "and when some little thing happened, it'd just turn 'em loose." Bergen worked on Alcatraz from September 1939, until June 1955, living on the island with his wife and two daughters. He became captain of the guards in 1949, and it was in this position that I met him as a child. As captain, he was tough, unassailable and respected—but not always liked. "Here lies Bergen under the grass," remembered one interviewee who saw the epithet written on an Alcatraz wall, "now the maggots can kiss his ass." Walking to his home on the parade ground after work in his dark uniform, his captain's hat hitched low over his eyes, he looked every bit the frightening, gruff man whose reputation preceded him. But years later when I knew him as an adult, I found him intelligent, thoughtful, and occasionally convinced by a well-reasoned argument. Although well into his eighties, he was still a strong spokesman for Alcatraz, which earned him even more jealousy from other former officers.

"I never struck the first blow or called them any obscene names," he said in a broadcast once about prisoners. His approach was simple and direct. "On the other hand, if a prisoner struck me, I never could entertain this idea of merely trying to restrain them. If I were struck, I struck back. And tried to strike back a little harder." Bergen saw it sometimes as a game to be played out:

They had a great big iron basket that was made in the shops [he said, in speaking of how inmates would get back at the guards]. And they hung that on the end of the sewer pipe [down at the bay]. Every once and a while the inmates would flush their clothes down the toilet. ...On one of the days when they were mad for some reason, you'd expect a general flushing of clothing. We'd take an [inmate] detail down and they'd pick all that crummy clothing out of the basket and take it back to the laundry and launder 'em and give it back to 'em. [He laughed heartily.] It's crazy, isn't it?

"You didn't go around hollering at them, 'Heh! You! This!'" said Bill Long. "They knew you got authority, so they're not going to fight. But if you go around and show your ass, then you're going to struggle all the way."

"You don't get cooperation out of a guy who hates your guts," said Isaac Faulk in speaking of the public's misconception about prison officers. Most officers soon learned to ignore petty infractions. If you were a guard who purposely messed up a con's good time, he resented it, and worse, he'd talk it up among his buddies. "And they're more organized than the guards are," Faulk said.

"I had inmates over the years working for me that I put more trust and confidence in than I did some of my fellow officers," said Marvin Orr, who worked there from 1939, until he retired in 1960. He told a story about one prisoner who jumped in front of another convict to protect Orr. " 'You get Orr after you get me'," he said the prisoner shouted.

An unknown Alcatraz prisoner humorously depicts glove shop supervisor Al Larmey as a convict.
(COURTESY OF ART DOLLISON)

Orr's story is not that unusual. A small, wiry man, with a face as deeply lined as a cracked river bed, he settled in the Bay Area after retiring from Alcatraz, and befriended several former prisoners. When one died, Orr and his wife went to his funeral, having known the man for many years. In that regard Orr wasn't that unique.

"I'd even take some of these old thugs—when I was up in Leavenworth—and bring 'em home and feed 'em," said Bud Mawbrey, former Alcatraz officer. Mawbrey (not his real name) had been in the U.S. Marines during World War II, and had earned the Navy Cross for heroism. That gave him a taste for being where the action was, and once the stateside Marines lost its excitement, he joined the prison service and served on Alcatraz from 1947, until 1960. He was a large, fearless man, described by one as a "damn good prison man," by others as intimidating and blustery. "Get permission from the warden and bring 'em home," he continued:

Officers and prisoners were convinced that the food on Alcatraz was the best in the federal prison system. The reasons may have been the small size of the institution, or because prisoners who get good food and plenty of it are more apt to stay put. Since favorite foods can be used as barter in prison, prisoners were allowed as much as they wanted.

(PHIL DOLLISON)

An official photograph taken in the late 1950s or early '60s, shows prisoners shielding their faces in the Alcatraz dining room. Note the musicians in the background—it may have been set up for the photographer or a holiday. The dining hall of any prison can be one of the most dangerous places for officers as well as prisoners. Here, there were tear gas canisters in the ceiling. (COURTESY OF PHIL DOLLISON)

I used to take 'em out and run 'em around town. Never been outside the institu-
tion in thirty years! I figured they wasn't going to do nothing I couldn't handle.
I took one feller, John Paul Chase, home for dinner. . . .I'd known him for twenty
years. [Florence Madigan Stewart said that he brought Chase to their home
one night.]

"You get a rapport with convicts," George Gregory said matter-of-factly. Gregory,
whose cynicism and battle experiences often matched those of prisoners, established
rapport through humor and a pragmatic realism. "And you don't ever tell a lie, see. They're
allowed to tell lies—that's part of the game. But you're breaking the rules if you lie."

"When I was coming up on the island," said Phil Dollison, "I never saw any tension
between guards and prisoners. I saw lots of inmates and guards working together, but I
never saw anyone being disrespectful, or condescended to, or yelled at. The public
consensus was that Alcatraz was a brutal prison, but it wasn't; prisoners ate the same food
as the guards, they were always clean, they looked sharp, and everyone was respectful of
one other."

It was the smart officer who treated prisoners fairly. "Either they respected you or they
did not," said Bill Rogers, who worked on "The Rock" from 1958, until it closed in 1963:

. . . If you were known as a guy who—in order to get back at an inmate—would
bum-rap him or plant something on him, God help you if the inmates ever took
over the cell house.

Brutality is a more highly charged word than violence. And if you ask was there brutality
at Alcatraz the answer would be yes—among the prisoners.

But there's a hitch that often sociologists and the public forget: prison brutality is
double-sided, moving in an always escalating retaliation. One provokes another. The
reasons for the escalation are as common as the tension.

"There could be a killing," said former prisoner Clarence "Joe" Carnes, "and it could
happen so easily—over nothing." He snapped his fingers for emphasis. "I have *seen* these
nothing things happen!" Carnes served at Alcatraz for eighteen years and was one of the
youngest men ever sent there. He was a naive, gullible, boyish Choctaw Indian from a dirt-
poor family in Oklahoma. Truancies and penny-ante stealing during the depression led

eventually to robbery of a gas station with a partner. Gun in hand, the robbers shot and killed the attendant. Despite having no previous arrests, he said, he pled guilty and received a life sentence in Oklahoma.

At Oklahoma State Reformatory in 1943, he ditched a rock quarry crew, ran away, coerced a driver to cross state lines, and got charged with what convicts call "technical kidnapping." Carnes later said he went three blocks and got five years. But that wasn't all: he pled guilty and got ninety–nine years for the kidnapping and five years for escape. He was sent to Leavenworth, then quickly to Alcatraz. Arriving in 1945, at age nineteen, he was a bitter, sullen, silent Indian with a chip on his shoulder. One year later, his participation in another escape attempt earned him another life sentence. He didn't leave Alcatraz until it closed in 1963. When we met in 1979, he had finally been released from prison. He was a sincere, thoughtful man who had lost his bitterness, and who took responsibility for his poorly played-out life. "Words just flare up," he said:

It could be a domino game or an argument on the handball court as to whether the ball is out. . .The method of dealing throughout their lives has been violence, so that's what they resort to.

. . .The thing where they drew straws on the yard, [he said of another incident in the late '50s when prisoners drew straws to decide who would kill another]. And then saw it through. He was knifed but he lived. . . .It symbolized the viciousness, the deadliness that you walked with all the time. . . .The cold thing about it is that Alcatraz had fewer people like that than any other major institution in the country. So you can picture what these other prisons are like.

"Outside, if you see someone being hurt," said Henry Floyd Brown in the visiting room at Kansas

D block was also stacked three tiers high. The regular, segregation cells above were larger. Of the fourteen floor cells, six had gate fronts as well as solid doors which, when closed, would leave a man in total darkness and silence. These were known as "the hole."
(PHOTO BY PHIL DOLLISON)

State Penitentiary in 1983 (Brown was at Alcatraz for three years in the early '50s), "it's just normal procedure to call the police. In prison, if you see a guy laying on the tier with his throat cut, why, you walk on by and ignore him. Because you don't know why he was killed and *he might'a needed killin'."*

Most brutality in prison is between inmates. Actual retaliation between officers and prisoners took on a less deadly but more humiliating tendency. Convicts could retaliate by shredding an officer's uniform, or his family's clothes in the laundry. "They'd razor blade the hell out of some of that stuff," Carnes said later.

But there were more degrading ways. "Guys in the hole from time to time," he began, "might give the officers a hard time:

And after all, there would almost always be someone down there who was a hardass. Now, I did this myself: take a shit and piss in the toilet and made a goo of it and put it in a paper cup [we] were allowed to drink with, and when the lieutenant opened the door, poured it right in his face. Me and Porkchop and K. was on a hunger strike. And we got mad one night. So they took our blankets. So when the lieutenant opened the door at 3:00 AM we hit him. He said, 'What have I done to you?' And K. said, 'Get the son-of-a-bitch again!' And he slammed the door and went. But they didn't do anything. I've seen them beat guys up that did that.

In fact, fights between prisoners and officers occurred most often because of D block. Also called the Treatment Unit, or TU, D block contained the cells variously called the "segregation," "isolation," "solitary," "dark," or "hole" cells. D block was walled off from the main population; men there did not eat or go to the yard with the others. Some stayed for years, having murdered a prisoner or guard, or having been involved in an escape attempt or caught in a violent, homosexual triangle. Others earned segregation for a shorter time, depending on the severity of their deed. Still others netted the Special Treatment Unit, or the "hole," the six dark cells, which, when fully closed, formed an isolation tank. One fought his way to the hole by decking an officer or by violent, repeated outbursts of anger. Hole time, according to Art Dollison, could last from one to nineteen days.

"A lot of times a prisoner don't want to go to the hole, see, and especially if he's mad," said former Lieutenant Faulk. "So you have to use force to do it."

"If they don't come out," said another officer, "we go and get 'em. That's part of the

It was possible for a man to go from a minimum security institution to Alcatraz in a short time. One man was first confined at the National Training School for Boys, then quickly progressed to Chillicothe, then Terre Haute, Lewisburg and Leavenworth—increasingly secure prisons—until he wound up at Alcatraz, serving for a time in the "hole." He was twenty-two years old.

job you signed on for."

The prisoner was usually the first to throw a fist. That he'd get slugged or beaten up because of it was a consequence he knew was probable; that he'd get thrown in the hole, especially if he continued to resist physically, was probable. He knew that if the next time an officer approached his cell he continued his vituperative outbursts, it would earn him tighter lockup. Not only the grill front but the solid door would shut, leaving him in total eclipse, isolated with just his own thoughts and sense deprivation. Further humiliation was possible, but it rested on the behavior of the inmate. Nonetheless, this is where the circumstance of prison violence and the charge of brutality to prisoners becomes cloudy.

"Some guards would probably be apprehensive," Clarence Carnes said:

Everybody there was doing so much time and on any given day he night decide to die. The officers were aware that they could only push you so far. It wouldn't be wise to come down on you very hard. They dealt with situations intelligently and unemotional for the most part. …That might be the reason why in all the years I was there they never beat me, never kicked me, because I was doing so much time. …I just might decide to commit suicide, take somebody with me.

But officers did talk guardedly of unnecessary violence. Bill Long recounted an event that occurred one Christmas during his years at Alcatraz:

I think it was breakfast, and pretty soon I looked up and the damn Christmas tree was going back though the mess hall. [Christmas was a difficult time for some prisoners, and evidently this man wanted it to be over.] Well . . . three officers grabbed him and about that time you heard this 'pop-pop-pop' and that was one of your gentlemen with the sap. [The] lieutenant was raining this guy's skull with about three or four shots with the sap, and—ah—the inmates really got up in arms about that. We're holding the guy and he's laying sap on him.

But other incidents were even less clear. "There was a man in a solitary cell, and he was using excrement, and every time the officer opened the door he'd throw it at the officer," Bud Mawbrey told me:

His cell was filthy, stinking, it was unsanitary. He used his excrement to mark

Clarence Carnes, AZ #714. Regarded as the youngest man ever transferred to Alcatraz, at age nineteen. He remained there seventeen years, from 1945 until 1963, and only transferred off because the island prison closed.

*the walls. So we went in to move him, to put him in a clean cell and give him a
bath, and he resisted us. . . .We had to control him. And there's only one way to
control him, that's to knock him out.*

*Otherwise there was three of us, and you're trying to hold a slimy guy covered
with crap, and take him down and shower him, and you just can't fight him all
the way. The best way is to put him out, put him in the shower, bathe him,
put him in a clean cell and when he wakes up, didn't hurt him. Boxer don't
get hurt when he gets knocked out. But—ah—the Bureau don't like that.
They frown on that . . .*

Prison men judge each other by their willingness or unwillingness to take part in such
confrontations. The tougher guards were disdainful of the majority of men who, as Bergen
put it, would "fade away" when a fight ensued. The men who avoided fights were
contemptuous of the small "goon squad" that existed to handle the rougher residents. But
in a dangerous situation they called on those men to help out.

It was a duplicitous arrangement that caused some officers to feel betrayed by their
colleagues in the end. "Every time they had trouble in a unit at Alcatraz, they'd say, 'Go
get Mawbrey.' So I was in on it, see?" Mawbrey said somewhat bitterly. "What'd they
say [in the end]? 'Well, he's just an old thug'."

"Sap's got a handle-like, and it's got a spring in the handle, and it's got buckshot or a piece of lead," said one officer. "The big reason they never said nothin' about 'em is because they was far less harmful than using a wooden billy or one of those gas billies."

But perhaps men judged each other less by the force they sometimes administered than
by the relish they displayed in administering it. "There was no brutality at Alcatraz," an
officer would say disdainfully. "Some of them got brutal in there," another would counter.
So it sometimes goes in a maximum security prison, especially when a warden doesn't
always know—*or want to know*—how officers handle prisoners.

But guards, said one prisoner, were *insane* about security, and shivs were the principal
reason. Knives made out of tableware, nail files, shanks of steel, halves of scissors, pen
parts, screwdrivers; knives with three and four-inch blades filed razor sharp; knives with
foot-long blades were the reason men were insane about security. Lives depended on it.

"I always started at the top," said George Gregory, who after the inmate orderlies were
released (they waxed and buffed the floors, painted cells and made minor repairs), would
fulfill a lieutenant's order to shake down cells:

I would take the books, rifle through them, 'cause they can often cut the pages

*out of the inside and hide things in there. And then I'd go through their clothing,
me-tic-u-lous-ly. Then their bed, of course. And also some beds had hollow legs
and you had to check on that because they could put stuff up [there]. And shake
every blanket down, and to the best you can, you'd check the mattress, especially
check for rips or a new sewing job. And also, we'd periodically take the mattress
out and run 'em through a metal detector, and change mattresses.*

*And the little air vent at the bottom [of the cell]?—check that to see if
strings hanging down, where they might have something tied on . . .*

Left: In the early years, prisoners were permitted very few items in their cells
and each item was noted by the cell house officer in charge. Although security
was always an issue, in later years this rule was relaxed a little and prisoners were
allowed more items in their cells. (NATIONAL MARITIME MUSEUM)

Right: Prisoners could change cells and did so frequently, to cell near a friend,
or away from someone, or for security reasons. Not infrequently, men moved
around to five or six different cells. (PHIL DOLLISON)

Five Alcatraz children (including me in the hat) stand before a fenced–in playground 1955. Parents worried about their children falling off cliffs, balconies or into the water more than they worried about prisoners. "Billy would be down at the beach and back before you'd know it," said Jean Long of her ten-year-old.

44

Life on "The Rock"

It was just like ants when the school boat whistle blew. Kids ran out of their apartments, across the big playground, down the steps by the side of 64 building and across the balcony; they plowed down the steep, terraced, concrete stairway between the balcony and the Dock tower, hitting the dock about the same time as the boarding whistle blew.

Most of us got pretty good at bouncing down those steps two and three at a time, while a silent and rather stern woman known as the "balcony lieutenant" watched daily from the railing of 64 building to make sure none of us fell into the bay.

Bill Dolby, who was nine years old when he moved on the island in the 1940s, used to wait until the last minute to run for the boat. "I was always cutting it close. So was my mother," he said. "The whistle would blow and that would be about the time we would dash out the door. I had those steps down pat and I could go down about six or seven at a time, full speed. I never fell, but I'd be the last on the boat, time after time."

Our lives were punctuated by the boat schedule, and the comings and goings of the broad-beamed, high-bowed cruiser, the *Warden Madigan,* an old Korean War offshore island steel supply boat converted for use at Alcatraz. In the last days of Alcatraz, the little launch made twenty–two round trips a day. The school boat was the 7:10 AM and by 3:30 or 4:10 PM, we were back on the boat for the twelve-minute ride home.

Dick Waszak was the boat lineman for awhile. His job, once the boat pulled into the dock, was to grab the line connected to the pier, tie up the boat and assist everyone in boarding. Waszak learned quickly that his was not always an easy task. "The lines? Yeah, [they] pulled me into the water and almost killed me there," he said:

We had already reached Fort Mason [where the boat later docked on the main-land]. The seas were real rough. I reached out with the gaff to get hold of the

*line and the boat went one way and the line went the other. I held onto the line
. . . and dropped between the boat and the float.*

"You have to understand," said Pat Mahoney, an Alcatraz officer who was the licensed boat operator for nearly four years of his six years on Alcatraz, "in those swells [a boat] can almost drop four feet. And Waszak was a very determined individual. He held onto that line. Well, it should have killed him."

*The boat come crashing back and I grabbed hold of one of the tires [attached to
the float, Waszak said] and shoved it up so it would force me into the water.
When that thing come crashing back against the dock it tipped my hat—the old
police hats we used to wear? And it went over my eyes. That's how close it came.
. . . I just swam around the corner and climbed up.*

Waszak was lucky; George Buell, who had the job of boat lineman in the mid-50s, said he broke a hip when he fell into the water and the boat crashed into him. About twenty years later part of his hip was surgically replaced.

A pulley-operated gangplank attached to the dock at Fort Mason and angled down to the float. Because the tide changed so radically the walkway needed to move up and down, sometimes as much as five or six feet. Often it hung in midair until someone walked on it or pulled it down to the floating platform where the boat moored.

"If you had bags and the tide was low!" Alma Ridlon declared, laughing. Alma was a German who immigrated to the United States after World War II and lived on Alcatraz with her husband, John, who manned the power house from 1960 until '63. They had two children, ages two and five:

*I would tell my kids to stay in the car. I would unload my bags. Then I went
down that gangplank which was about four feet off the platform, so it stood
way up high and you grabbed it, and your weight and the groceries got it
right down. You dropped your bag quick and ran back before it would go up
again [she laughed]. You do that a couple of times. . . . Then of course
you waited for the boat.*

"On two or three memorable occasions there was no float and no plank to walk," recalled Phyllis McPherson Weed, whose stepfather, "Mac" McPherson worked on Alcatraz from 1942 until 1960:

Then the launch tied up tight against the pilings of the pier, and we climbed the ladder slats nailed to the pilings. Because such ladders were rarely used they were in poor repair. Some slats were loose, some missing altogether. And the damp, slime, tar and oil were hard on high heels, nylon hose, good clothes and clean hands. The last scramble over the raised edge of the pier totally destroyed any remaining shred of dignity.

In fact, dignity figured into a lot of encounters islanders had with the bay. Maryanne Waszak thought for a moment, then asked, "Whose color television went into the water?"

"That was 1959," Mahoney remembered later, chuckling. The *Warden Madigan* was not in service yet. Instead, the old *Warden Johnston,* a low-slung, beamy, class-T boat built especially for Alcatraz and used for most of the years it was a federal penitentiary, was in operation. A custodial officer had just purchased an eight-hundred dollar color console with a ninety-dollar service guarantee. Mahoney called it "the first color television set on Alcatraz." The man and his son were carrying it down the gangplank when the float moved out from under them and the TV set plunged into the drink, the kid with it. "Well, the float came back and it would have crushed the kid," Mahoney said, "but instead the TV set got crushed." Mahoney didn't know how they got the set out of the water or how damaged it really was; he arrived on the Fort Mason dock minutes later, seeing a shivering kid and a chagrined father. A year later, when the officer was transferred, Mahoney bought

Residents disembark from the boat while a guard, temporarily assigned, assists. (PHIL DOLLISON)

the set for $250-350, he said, and used it for the next ten years.

Dozens of stories circulated about people accidentally dropping items in the water while getting on or off the boat. One man, carrying a brand new bunk bed mattress—still wrapped in paper—dropped it in the bay. "Yeah, and the tide was going out!" he said, remembering his panic. He retrieved it with a gaff. Another story was often told of a man whose wife slipped and fell in, ladened with a case of beer. Alcoholic beverages were against the employee rules on Alcatraz, but the man didn't hesitate. When his wife bobbed back up to the surface, he yelled, "Give me the beer! The beer!"

But most trips were uneventful. The little boat slowly thumped and jumped through the white caps, avoiding the freighters and sailboats, returning to Alcatraz. Rounding the east side of the island, one could see the large "WARNING, U.S. PENITENTIARY" sign which kept other boats from coming too close to the island prison. Nearby, always just outside the two–hundred-yard marking buoys, were the bay cruisers filled with tourists. They rounded the island constantly while hundreds of people, binoculars in hand, crowded to one side, attempting to see what they could on Alcatraz. It always seemed as if those boats listed to starboard.

"You'd hear this speaker," said LuAnne Freeman, who stood on the balcony of 64 with Betty Miller one day, waiting for her kids to return. "We didn't hear the whole spiel because of the wind , except that 'Those women on the island were really families of the inmates.' Betty was ready to walk on water to clarify that!"

Life on Alcatraz was not so restrictive in the late 1950s and early 1960s when the boat ran as often as a bus. Earlier, only eleven round trips went a day, and earlier still only seven or eight, and that demanded a thousand little changes in one's daily habits.

Commuting by boat was not conducive to making large household purchases either. People assembled their babies, their books and groceries, sometimes their Christmas trees or their new lamps, and got ready to disembark from a slippery deck to a tar-papered gangplank up to the island dock. During workdays, about six or seven prisoners lined up on the other side of the dock, waiting for us to pass before returning to work.

The boat waited for no one; that was the rub. The last scheduled trip of the night was the midnight run; later a 2:00 AM boat existed if a request came in soon enough. But teenagers, especially, were loathe to call the Control Center from the mainland (few families had telephone connections to the city) to request it, because the Control Center officer called your parents as well. And the 2:00 AM option had only been a recent innovation. "You had

"They used to say that a haircut cost 'em five dollars," said Marvin Orr. "In those days they were fifty cents. But when they got through with the cut they had to wait for the boat, and they'd go to a bar, and by the time they'd catch the boat, it'd cost 'em five bucks."

to be back by the last boat or you stayed over," my brother Phil Dollison said once with a slight catch in his voice, remembering back to when he was a teenager on the island and no other boat left after midnight. "And sometimes that worked to your benefit and sometimes that worked to your detriment."

Many kids remembered a few days when the seas were so rough the warden decided to give everyone a school holiday. Parents called the schools from pay phones on the island and the kids gladly stayed home. Dolby remembered one such day; he and a friend sneaked on the boat and rode it back and forth all morning.

"They had some pretty rough rides," remembered Fred Mahan, "and sometimes our boat would get lost in the fog and we would have to ring the bell on the dock and the officers would have to go down on the shoreline and guide [it] in.

The mouth of the Golden Gate is one of the largest breaks in the California coastal mountains and provides a lane for storms and fog to pass into the bay. Indeed, much of the heaviest fog, occurring in summer, is sucked in by weather patterns about eighty miles northeast of San Francisco. The Sacramento River Valley heats up and, when the hot air rises, it attracts cool air from the ocean through the Golden Gate.

"When the fog came in," Dolby said, "it wasn't just a little mist:

It was solid—roll right in. That coming right in under the Gate, and ships disappearing right into that fog bank. [One time] we started towards the island. Well, the fog around the island was overwhelming. Literally you couldn't see twenty feet. It was thick! We couldn't see the island. We went around several times, all the kids had life preservers on, people all over the island, yelling, 'This isn't it, you're at the beach, go back the other way.' We could hear 'em yelling. It took us about an hour-and-a-half.

"Oh my God!" exclaimed Alma Ridlon, "we got there in August and the fog started rolling in, and the blinds rattled and the bed vibrated! I could *not* sleep! [They lived about a hundred feet from a foghorn.] I used to count it. It was thirty seconds after mine blew that the other one blew on the other end. . . . After six months I got used to the foghorn."

Dick and Maryanne Waszak had been living in Omaha, Nebraska, when he applied for the job and took the civil service exam:

Bill Long came to get us and he said, 'I want you to see what it looks like.

People live there,' [Maryanne began]. I wasn't going to go. That was the most frightening experience of my life. Just the thought of walking onto that island.

They moved onto the island in November 1959. "We had no choice," she explained. "There was no survival in San Francisco." Dick was a junior officer and had a civil service rating of GS-6; he was making $4480 a year (or $2.15 an hour). "The day we moved on he worked the four–to–midnight shift:

We got to the island, our furniture was on the dock, we got one bed up and he took off [she continued]. I did not know how to light the gas stove. I had to feed the kids. . . . It was like I was a stranger from a foreign land. And when he got home at midnight, we went down on the dock and he and I carried the furniture up.

They moved into 64 building, a former Army barracks which had been converted to family quarters and was by then a dismal apartment building. Twenty-seven apartments made up the three-story stone edifice that rose from the wharf. Because of the conversion, it had blind halls, dead-end stairways and blocked-up fireplaces.

My father moved into 64 building in 1953, and we followed a few months later. Like most everyone, we awaited our turn to move into the newer apartments across the parade ground in buildings A, B and C. In 1955, though, my parents bought a house in a San Francisco suburb and my father commuted to work. (We returned to the island for one more year in November, 1961, when my father became the associate warden, and lived in the more gracious, Spanish-style duplex at the east end of the island.) Although some corner apartments were large and well-positioned for an exquisite view, few people liked 64. The apartments were dingy.

Dick and Maryanne carried their furniture up the seven flights of stairs to their apartment on the first balcony.

"I weighed ninety–eight pounds," Maryanne said. "We had an *Amana* freezer that he and I carried up together."

"We had a washer and a dryer," he remembered.

Waszak eventually worked in federal prisons in Florida, Kansas, and Tennessee before he retired in 1980. Maryanne was by then working in real estate, and their children were grown. Dick's red hair had turned a little lighter by then, but he still had his sunny disposition. "I fell apart after I retired," he kidded later. Like many prison officers who are under a lot of stress, he suffered several heart attacks and waited out a long recovery. He continued, remembering the day they moved on:

We moved into an apartment [in 64] and then we moved up to what they called the 'Cow Palace,' an eleven-room apartment on the third floor of the building. It was a biggie.

"People on the island were getting a big break," said Officer Bill Rogers, who lived with his wife and family near the Waszaks at that time. "You got your apartment furnished with the utilities paid for twenty–five dollars a month. There's no way you could beat that. Not

Evelyn Dollison stands in 1962 at the associate warden's residence on one of the few patches of grass on Alcatraz, with the warden's residence and lighthouse in the background. (JOLENE BABYAK)

in San Francisco."

If you took marbles or a ball [Maryanne continued] and you rolled them from the opposite end of the apartment, they would all roll towards the middle. [We paid] twenty–one dollars a month."

"Everything was paid," Dick said, "plus we got our laundry done free."

They had an old torn-up apartment right there at the corner [Rogers continued]. That was your break-in. A lot of people had to live in that until something else came open. It was nearly always open because everyone was so anxious to get out of it. It was a real rat-hole. My wife cried when I showed it to her the first time. Then a fellow resigned and we had a real nice apartment.

The dark alley at the fort level below 64 building, known from the Army prison-era as "Chinatown." Rumors among the kids had it that Army prisoners in the early 1860s were confined in cells here, but there is no evidence of that.
(PHOTO BY PHIL DOLLISON)

Electricity was the biggest inconvenience on the island. Although Alcatraz generated its own power, the old diesel engine pumped out direct current. It could be counted on to blow toasters, irons, vacuum cleaners, TVs or stereos, often the moment they were plugged in. So alternating converters were purchased in the city. "Converters were a premium," Dick remembered:

And it appeared to me that while the Chief of Mechanical Service was telling every-body that you can't have converters because it draws too much on the DC system, it was kind of prestigious to have a nice big converter. And if you were in that inner circle you could have your big converter. Well, Al Severson was getting transferred and Al had a big converter for his organ. And I thought, by golly, if he can have a converter for his organ, I can have a converter to wash diapers. Okay, we had a washer and a dryer but we obviously couldn't use them. Maryanne used the Amana freezer as a linen closet because we couldn't use that. We found a Maytag wringer washer with a DC motor on it and we used that until finally it died. So I packed it on my back one day, marched it out of 64 building, down the stairs to the dock and just deposited it right in the water. The tower man thought I'd gone bananas.

Waszak bought the converter and he and Pat Mahoney installed it after midnight one night so the CMS wouldn't catch them:

We put the washer and dryer in one of the bathrooms because it was a huge monstrous thing [Dick said]. And the converter was too big to be lugging it from room to room, [so] if we wanted waffles, we went into the bathroom and made our waffles.

I used to mash my potatoes in there [Maryanne said].

Fred "Fritz" Freeman was twenty–five years old when he and LuAnne, twenty–four, moved on the island in 1959. They had four children.

"It was spooky because we came over after hours one day to look at the apartment, and you know how 64 building looked," said LuAnne, rolling her eyes. "It didn't look like your Nob Hill apartments. But we were made to believe we were *very* fortunate to get it because there were so many on the waiting list."

Fred Freeman had been in the Yuba City, California sheriff's department when he took the civil service exam for the appointment at Alcatraz. It was his first prison assignment. The year they moved on the island, Fred said, he just skirted being knifed in a cell house incident and it scared him enough to quit. He was out fourteen months but kept thinking that if others could tough it out, so could he. He returned and remained with the federal prison service until retirement in January, 1983. We talked the summer before he retired in their home on the reservation of the U. S. Penitentiary at Terre Haute, Indiana. It was their sixth prison:

Family members needed keys to get in and out of the gates that surrounded our area. The alley known as "Chinatown" is two stories below the railing at right.
(CORINNE EDWARDS)

*I had a different attitude when we came back [LuAnne said]. I think both of us
had learned a lot. As far as being afraid, I kept my doors locked, and I don't
here. I didn't at Leavenworth and we had trash men come. I didn't at Texarkana,
and heavens, we had yard men there. I think [it has] to do with maturing a little.
But I didn't worry about the children on the island because we knew the only
inmates out were on the dock.*

*One time I was scared. I came out on the balcony [of 64] and went up on the
second balcony to go to Betty Howell's for a permanent. Fred was the dock
officer that day, and as I walked out an inmate nudged Fred and Fred looked at
me. I remember him doing it. And when he came home that night, I said, 'How
did that inmate know?' And he said, 'Honey, they know more about us than
you'd believe.'*

Everyone had similar stories. My father thought it uncanny that prisoners could learn
so much so fast. Whenever agents from the Federal Bureau of Investigation (FBI) landed—
in those days when J. Edgar Hoover was director they were easy to recognize in their dark,
impeccably tailored suits—prisoners over the island knew it before they got to the prison,
he said. Mary McCreary Duggal, who was a teenager on the island when I lived there, said
that a popular song one year contained the lyrics "All night, all day Mary Anne…" and she
was embarrassed once hearing an inmate worker whistling the tune near her apartment.

*All the women on the island—and I knew most of them [said LuAnne Free-
man]—it was none of this smiling at them or anything else. The inmates didn't
even attempt to speak to you—they just didn't.*

  Unlike other prisons and farms where unattended trusties work outside the fence or near
the staff housing, there were no trusties on Alcatraz. Occasionally an island pickup truck
passed by with a guard at the wheels and two inmates on the sideboards, but even then
a fence stood between them and us. We were not permitted to talk to each other. We didn't
have to be told. My childhood feelings of awe and hushed reverence became more
complicated as I grew older and returned to the island as a fifteen–year–old. I felt
embarrassed for them and tried not to look at them.
  Nonetheless, all prisoners start to look the same after a while. You don't look long

Alcatraz kids went to school in San Francisco. There had never been a school on
the island, because everyone felt the kids
would be too isolated in the midst of the
San Francisco Bay Area.

(PRINTED IN COLLIER'S MAGAZINE, AUG.1954;
WILLIAM R. WOODFIELD, PHOTOGRAPHER)

enough, especially if you are a teenage girl, to notice facial features, the cut of the chin, who looked like a con, who was handsome. Prisoners dressed the same, had the same caps, the same Navy pea coats, the same, it seemed, searching eyes.

A modicum of contact did occur, however. I remember one dock inmate who used to bow with a theatrical flourish while tipping his hat whenever he saw one of the kids on the 64 balcony. Some boys had more contact with prisoners than others of us. That was not without repercussions, however, as Dolby showed in another account:

Kids weren't supposed to have toy guns over there, and I had a sort of a silhouette of a toy gun. I forget if we made it, but it didn't really qualify as a toy gun in my point of view. I dropped it over the balcony onto the dock, so I called down to one of the cons—said, 'Say, can you get that for me?' And I took a fishing line and lowered it down to the dock and had him hook it on and about the time he was hooking my gun onto the fishing line [Associate Warden] Miller walks along. He sees this con fumbling with a gun and he got a little excited over that! I think that particularly realistic–looking silhouette I was told to get rid of. It didn't really qualify as a non–toy gun.

Although there were often prisoners working near us, they were always accompanied by an officer and forbidden from making contact with the wives or children. (PHOTOGRAPHER UNKNOWN)

Seemingly ordinary concerns took on exaggerated meaning on an island prison. Garbage could not be discarded simply. Inmates were restricted to few reading materials, so residents' newspaper and magazines had to be bundled and put out with the laundry on Saturday morning rather than thrown in the garbage. Neither could cutlery, razor blades, saw blades or other tools, bottles, glassware or clothing be randomly thrown away. Such things were thrown in the bay.

Firearms, of course, were the greatest hazard. Personal firearms were kept in the Control Center, and officers had to be reminded from time to time not to carry pocket knives. Toy guns and water pistols were strictly forbidden.

LuAnne Freeman recalled an incident that occurred

right after they moved on the island. Their neighbors, the Millers, had a little boy named Skip. (Harold Miller, his wife Betty and their children lived on the island in the last years while he was a junior officer. Nearly twenty years later he was warden at the U.S. Penitentiary at Marion, Illinois—the prison that replaced Alcatraz.) "My daughter, Patty, was a brand new little neighbor so Skip promptly went in and under his bed pulls out this wooden toy pistol that he had no business having:

Of course Harold allowed him to have it under penalty of death if he took it out the door. Well, as kids will do, he went barreling out of his house with that pistol and Patty was right behind him. And of all places for him to go, he went right on the lower tier of 64 building, down by the post office. And who should be standing there, as usual, but the 'balcony lieutenant.' She took the gun and the kids came back crying. . . .Well, Fred figured he was fired for sure.

Locked fences were a part of everyone's lives. (CORINNE EDWARDS)

[That woman] was totally efficient and she did end up being a lieutenant. She went into the prison service after her husband passed away. She started at Terminal Island and the last we heard of her she was a lieutenant at Alderson. But she was as good as gold. She gave free ice cream every Saturday morning during the summer, and we never knew for the longest time who was paying for it. The kids all got free ice cream. But I was totally afraid of that woman. . . . She knew who went on the bus, who went on the boat, and who came home.

She always wore a fur coat with thongs, and her hair was cut with no curl to it. She usually had a cigarette and a cigarette holder. I could draw a picture of her, because I was young and had those four kids and I wasn't afraid of her, I just wanted to give her as wide a berth as possible because she didn't radiate friendship to me. She was real different. But I understand she made a fantastic officer, which doesn't surprise me. . . . She took that gun away from those kids and I proceeded after her and I said, 'It's not yours!' And she said, 'It's going up top!' and Betty kept yelling that we were gonna' get fired . . . And she called up top and they sent George Black after it. Well, the gun never made it up top.

Left: Electrician Frank Brunner walks from the warden's residence towards the prison building. The warden's residence, built in 1929 as the Military Commanding Officer's quarters, was of lovely California Mission-style architecture. Note the snow tracks on the concrete and roof. The photo was probably taken in 1961 when it briefly snowed on Alcatraz.

(COURTESY OF PHIL DOLLISON)

Right: Although Alcatraz was mostly rock and concrete, the trees and shrubs planted during the military post days flourished in the moist, fresh air.

(PHOTO BY JOLENE BABYAK)

LuAnne learned other lessons through her children. Prisoners' didn't have many visitors. Many men had lost contact with their families. Most were from the Midwestern or eastern states and family members couldn't travel so far for an hour–and–a–half visit every month. When they did show up, they were easily recognizable on the boat or on the squat blue bus that took them up top. The ones I saw were quiet, distant and usually alone. There were no kids. They may have been afraid of us—the staff kids—or a little embarrassed. Then too, they may have in fact been coping with a boat full of children. Nonetheless, there was little contact between us and them, though many of us were curious about them:

Patty and June and I were riding up on the bus [LuAnne began], and this sharp-looking girl—she was in her early twenties and very, pretty. I didn't see the diamond on her finger, but having a young daughter, she did. So the girls whispered to me, 'Who's that?' And I, from past exposure, said that it was Mickey Cohen's girlfriend. The kids were all in school and they were old enough to know who he was because that was prison talk around the house. So June meanders up the aisle of the bus before I could get her, and she said to this girl with the diamond ring, 'Did Mickey buy that for you?' I was just destroyed!

The gallows humor, the restrictions of island living and the notoriety of Alcatraz all reinforced the bonds that brought us together. To be sure, life on "The Rock" was restrictive: two–thirds of the island was off limit to us; families weren't permitted to have dogs or cats and the boat schedule never seemed convenient.

Because some guards worked the early morning hours and slept during the day, kids weren't permitted to play in the building hallways despite the often cold weather. We weren't allowed to go to the dock except to get on the boat, we were seldom permitted beyond the fence, up near the prison or down by the sea. That put us on the parade ground. "Touch football," said Dolby. "That was really exciting on concrete." Little kids had tricycles; few of the older ones had bikes—there was no place to go. Now and then a kid got to go up to the lighthouse and crank up the light.

Sometimes the most vivid memories of island living were the smallest ones. All the kids remember collecting bumblebees or trapping the fat, doleful slugs in jars and pouring salt on the. "Oh God! The slugs!" exclaimed one women who lived there during the 1950s. "That's about all I remember about Alcatraz."

The camaraderie shared by officers was also felt by islanders, however, and sometimes that spilled out onto the parade ground. The kids were used to seeing their dads walk down from prison in their dark uniforms. Although some men had difficulty losing the officiousness that permeated their working day, others never lost their insouciance, especially around kids. I can remember one dad coming down the hill in his dark uniform, ceremoniously taking off his prison jacket, hitting a baseball and running around the bases before begging off with a mock complaint about his advanced age. Phyllis Hess, who lived on Alcatraz from 1934 until 1938 remembered the day her dad, George Hess, M.D., the Chief Medical Officer, and Captain Henry Weinhold decided she should learn to fly a kite. "They became so engrossed in flying it themselves that they forgot I was there," she said. "I just sat down, amused, and watched two usually dignified men romping around, yelling, 'Heh, look what I made it do!'" At Christmas time, dads could been seen helping the younger children learn to ride their bikes, or giving us pointers on fly casting.

But mostly kids looked for ways to entertain themselves.

"We used to walk on the balcony [railing]," said Dolby, when asked what he did for fun. "You know—tightrope walk. One side was about three feet down and the other side was two stories down. The man in the tower, god, I guess he was afraid to yell."

Popsicle sticks served as toy guns [he continued]. Instead of playing cops and robbers, we played prison. And we'd set up an area, play prison and have big break-outs. Eight or ten of us. You know, the 'guards' had guns and what the guards used for guns and what you tried to conceal when you got in so you could make your break and stuff, was a popsicle stick.

. . . Before I had my key [to the gates which let him up top to deliver newspapers], I

Alcatraz teenagers and their friends pose at an island Christmas party in 1949. We were allowed to bring friends to the island as long as we met them at the San Francisco dock and escorted them over.
(COURTESY OF PAT BERGEN ROTHSCHILD)

discovered—now here's the world's total high security prison—I discovered you could unlock those locks with a popsicle stick. You shoved a stick in there, twisted it and it opened the lock. I called Miller or Madigan and said, 'I think there's something you might be interested in. . .' [He laughs.] I gave 'em a demonstration and about two days later all the locks were changed.

"We worried about the kids, sure" said Jean Long, wife of Bill Long and the island postmistress for many years. "Billy would be down at the beach and back before you'd know it," she said of her ten-year-old.

Mike Pitzer in many ways typified a teenager on the island who looked for ways to entertain himself:

A lot of times we would go down [to the beach] and wave the sailboats to come past the markers. In fact, one time one came in and the guards kept yelling at the guy and he kept sailing in, and there was a whole bunch of people on his boat and they were drinking and stuff and waving and we were yelling at them. 'Cause that was one of our big jokes, to try to get the boats to come [past the two–hundred–yard marker]. Usually the [tower guard] would just get on the horn and warn them. But this group kept coming in and coming in. We started yelling, 'Go Back! Go back!' after we saw they were going to come all the way in, you know. Then the guard fired a couple of warning shots. One of them hit the main sail and just ripped it right down the center. Then they turned around.

Pitzer also told of an incident in which he and another teenaged boy climbed the rocks along the shore towards the Golden Gate Bridge side of the island—an area strictly off-limits. The boys were caught and hauled into the warden's office where they were "chewed out," he said. It was easy to understand their discomfort; the warden of Alcatraz could be a formidable man and definitely had the power to kick families off the island. More important, however, was driving home the point that it was dangerous to wander around and be mistaken for escapees. "The lieutenant said that if the [tower officer] had been a younger guard, he would have probably opened fire on us." It was right after the June 1962 escape. The boys got the point.

There were rewards to living on Alcatraz, and the water figured into much of that. Swimming was out because of the strong currents and the numbingly cold temperatures, but there was fishing, and plenty of it. One photograph taken on Alcatraz in 1957 shows six men posed on the parade ground with approximately thirty striped bass in hand.

"Oh, they used to catch those bass there," Marvin Orr said, remembering the particularly famous incident. "I was on duty one night:

> *It was acting lieutenant and coming down the sea wall on the west side of the island about 2:00 in the morning. I threw my flashlight down in the water and you could see 'em. That water was just wiggling with bass. And I called Fred Mahan—he was quite a fisherman—and Fred called some other guys that like to fish and they came down and fished till daylight and they caught enough bass that night—the next morning they brought a pickup truck down there and filled it full. And fed the main line [of the prison population].*

"Jeez, we just went hog wild," said Mike Pitzer. "I never caught so many fish in my life. There were quite a few of us down there 'cause I remember when they brought the dump truck down to haul all those fish up there."

"The sardines would come in," said Orr, "and the bass would follow 'em in, see:

> *And those runs would only last about three hours, and when the sardines're gone, the bass're gone. And when daylight broke, these guys all along the bank, fishing you know, just—boy! you'd cast and you couldn't miss. You'd just pull them in just as fast as you could cast.*

> *And these fishing boats outside the buoys [the San Francisco fishermen fleet]. There's no bass out there! And those guys are just going crazy out there! They're trying to edge in. The officer in the tower motioning—chasing them back, you know. They were just having a fit out there!*

"I mean it was as fast as you could put your line out," said Long. "You could *not* get your line back without a fish on it:

> *It was the best one hour of fishing I had in my life. We actually had a pickup truck and we wheeled the fish out on a wheelbarrow up to where we could get a truck and took them to the dock and gave everybody all the fish they wanted*

there, and took the rest of them up and we fed the inmates all the fish they
could eat.

And so it went. For much of the twenty–nine years Alcatraz was a federal prison, life
for us "involuntary inmates" was surprisingly placid. Our island life was similar to other
neighborhoods in most ways. The city was close by and convenient. We commuted by
boat, of course, instead of bus, but that was the major difference. And perhaps because of
the sheer fortitude of the "balcony lieutenant," none of us ever fell into the bay.

Alcatraz residents, of course, talked about crime and criminals the way other people
talked about the weather. Maybe it helped ease anxieties, and keep the feelings of anxiety
at a distance. But the 1950s and 60s, unlike the decades before or after, were not times of
hostage-taking, after all. It may have occurred to some prisoners, Carnes once said, but it
was an idea quickly rejected. No one thought he'd get off the island alive with hostages.

And although Alcatraz had such an irreparably bad reputation, the kids took pride in
their fathers' work—and for good reason. When my brother Phil Dollison was a teenager
and living on the island, about thirty teenagers were in residence and at least ten of them
went into law enforcement as a career. Several started out working at San Quentin State
Prison, then moved into police work. Phil worked at San Quentin while he organized his
own burglar alarm business in San Francisco. "I had one guy in San Quentin—an inmate
who had been at Alcatraz—tell me he'd much rather be in Alcatraz than San Quentin," Phil
said. "He told me at least there he knew where he stood."

Our lives were not unlike those in the military service. Perhaps because our fathers felt
that few outsiders understood their problems, prison people often remained insulated.
Vacations in our household tended to include tours to other prisons where battle stories
were relived—an endlessly tedious practice in my mind then. And although our fathers
only walked a few hundred yards to work in one of the most notorious cell houses in the
nation, we gave little thought to the purpose of "The Rock" as anything other than our
home. Except sometimes:

I was working as captain's clerk [said Dick Waszak]. After the four o'clock
count we were to feed the inmates and it was precarious because all the inmates
would be in the dining room at that time and if any problems were to start, not
only was staff down, but you'd have all the inmates out. And Blackwell was

(L. to R.) Lloyd Miller, Ira Bowden, Bill Long, Calvin Roster, unidentified, and Dwayne Blackwell. Among them are more than thirty striped bass. Fishing from Alcatraz was one of the benefits of the job on Alcatraz. (PHOTOGRAPHER UNKNOWN; COURTESY OF JOHN BRUNNER)

warden and he was also working late this one night and the three-deuce alarm went off. . . . That's the standard alarm. . . . And of course any time the alarm goes off, your adrenalin starts pumping.

. . . So I jumped over a railing, got to the phone and answered it and I could hear what sounded like kids in the background. Obviously it was somebody playing with the phone. So I fussed at them for a moment and told them to get off the phone. And seconds later it rang a second time. And of course my reaction was the same. You're really not sure whether someone's playing games or whether we actually have a problem. And I could still hear these kids. I made the comment to the warden that, by gosh, if they were my children, I'd sure take care of things. About that time the three-deuces goes off again, and I said, 'You kids get off this telephone!' I says, 'Now who is this?' And a little guy on the other end says, 'This is Mike, Daddy, will you come play with me?' And it was my own son!

We didn't actively *worry* about escapes—except sometimes. "When they had a call for an emergency up top," said Bill Long, "everybody went just the way they were:

When we had a disturbance, [if] we were at a party, we didn't put on coats or anything, we just went right up the hill. They used to call down at 64 building and the phone was right outside my apartment and we answered the phone and they'd say, 'We have trouble in the cell house,' and that's all they had to say. Everybody available went. . . . They'd hit the deuces and the deuces would go off and the Control Center man would make a decision what to do. . .

Four Alcatraz children, identified as Bob Orr, Don Faurot, Don Martin and O.P. Flynt, sit atop one of the Rodman cannons left over from the military post days.

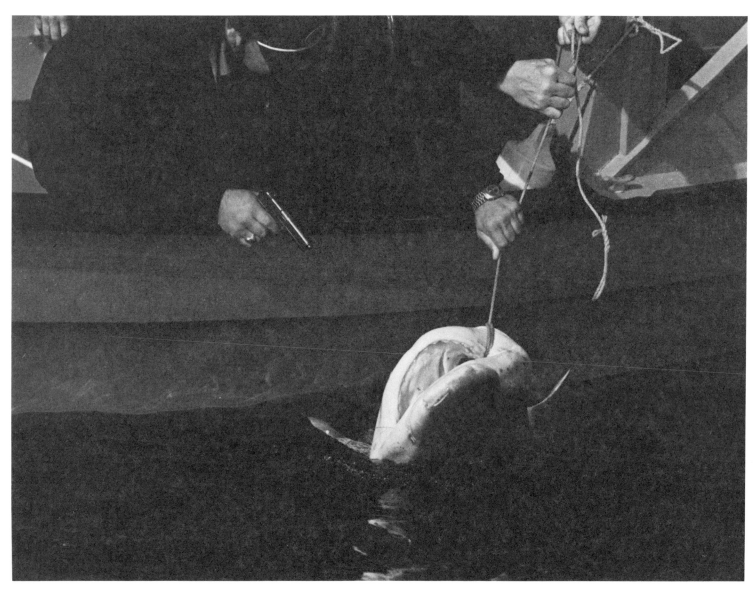

Sharks are as common in San Francisco Bay as rumors about them were among prisoners. But they were not considered dangerous to bay swimmers. This photo, taken in San Francisco Bay in 1980, shows a fisherman intent on killing a shark before bringing it aboard. (JOLENE BABYAK)

Escape Attempts
1934-1946

December, 1937

"You know what kind of characters you had up there," George Steere said, "but when that old siren takes off, you didn't know what was going on." Steere, twelve years old at the time, had lived on the island about a year when the first escape siren sounded. (This was the second attempt from the prison, but the first in which convicts made it as far as the bay. Joe Bowers, AZ #210, the first man to attempt escape, was climbing a perimeter fence when he was warned and then shot by a tower guard on April 27, 1936. He fell to his death. Many were convinced it was actually a suicide attempt.)

Steere's home was the old Army hospital up by the prison which was torn down in the early 1940s. "Our dining room used to be the operating room," he said many years later. "We were right outside the prison, by the morgue."

The siren sounded on December 16, 1937. Theodore Cole, #AZ 258, a small twenty–three–year–old man convicted of kidnapping and transferred from Leavenworth on the same shipment as Ralph Roe, #AZ 260, a twenty–nine–year–old man convicted of bank robbery reportedly doing ninety–nine years, broke out of an industrial shop, dropped down to the bay, and vanished.

"Blackie" Audett claimed to have been watching from the other end of the shop when he saw them jump from the window. He wrote in his book that he saw Ralph Roe hit the water and come up about twenty–five yards later, already floundering, and then watched him disappear into a fog bank just as the prison siren screamed out the escape attempt.

Steere knew instinctively what to do. He didn't go outside. He sat, waiting, with a baseball bat in his hand.

Joyce Rose Ritz was on a city bus returning to Alcatraz from junior high school in San Francisco when she saw an early newspaper headline. By that time, down at the bottom on Van Ness Avenue, where the boat docked in those early days, a guard was waiting for all kids to assemble. "They were always afraid of the kids being kidnapped so they kept a pretty good watch on us." Ritz said. "The little ones used to go to school in a cab."

After what seemed like an terminally long boat ride, she and other children whose mothers were working in the city were herded into a house by a guard and told to stay put. Every man men had gone to the prison. Everyone else stayed inside and stayed off the island telephones. It was a tense time; residents were now prisoners in their own homes until the escapees were located, or determined to be off the island.

"We were sitting, talking, and suddenly I looked up and saw the door open—we were all petrified—and two of us girls dove underneath the kitchen table, another ran into the bedroom. One of the older boys picked up a big piece of wood and [ran] to the door—ready to hit someone." Joyce Ritz would hear the Alcatraz siren sound a few more times before she moved off the island in 1951. But this was her first experience. She laughs about it now. The door slowly opened on the frightened children, and a friendly face appeared. It was an officer, making the mandatory search of each apartment.

Officers continued searching for about a week, but Roe and Cole were never heard from again. No bodies; no fingerprints. They simply vanished.

In its twenty–nine–year federal prison history, Alcatraz held fifteen–hundred–seventy–six prisoners. Thirty–six of them—in fourteen events— got out of the buildings and down to the shore. Of those, twenty–one were returned alive, seven were killed by gun fire, one drowned and his body washed ashore and two were returned and executed.

Five are still missing—Roe and Cole in 1937 and Frank Morris and Clarence and John Anglin in 1962.

May, 1938

Five months later, on May 23, another escape attempt occurred. James C. Lucus, #AZ 224, serving thirty years for bank robbery and kidnapping, Thomas Limerick, #AZ 263, on a life sentence for bank robbery and kidnapping, and Rufus "Whitey" Franklin, #AZ 335, doing thirty years for bank robbery, caught Officer Royal Cline in a disadvantaged

Prisoners leaving the Industries area, which was contained in two buildings—the "new" Industries, left foreground, and the old model building in the background. Each day they walked through several metal detectors. (COURTESY OF PHIL DOLLISON)

Alcatraz was not a rehabilitative prison; men had lost that privilege by being transferred here. Prison Industries was almost an afterthought. Shops generally handled one or two military or government contracts at a time, or in the case of the brush, and the glove shop, above, were satellites of the main factories in the U.S. prisons at Leavenworth, Kansas and Danbury, Connecticut. (PHIL DOLLISON)

moment. Lieutenant Isaac Faulk later speculated that Officer Cline was talking to another prisoner, because he was hit in the back of the head with a claw hammer. "They sunk that right in his skull," Faulk said. The trio got nowhere for their troubles. Limerick was fatally shot in the head storming the Model tower; Lucas and Franklin gave up and were eventually tried. Cline, however, was dead.

Now a veteran of two escape attempts on Alcatraz, Joyce Ritz found it all very exciting. A subtle change occurred among the children of the guards, however. Cline had kids. His death drove home the realization that it could happen to anyone's father.

January, 1939

Federal prison officers only made $1680 a year in the 1930s, whether they worked a minimum security prison or a hardship post like Alcatraz. The fourth escape attempt in thirty–three months occurred on January 13, 1939. This time the escape siren sounded at about 2:30 AM.

Five men, serving a combined two–hundred–and–twenty–nine years, had sawed out of their segregation cells, then spread the bars of a cell block window. Arthur "Doc" Barker, #AZ 268, serving life for kidnapping, Dale Stamphill, #AZ 435, life for kidnapping, Henri Young, #AZ 244, serving two twenty–year sentences for armed bank robbery, William Martin, #AZ 370, an African–American man serving twenty years for post office robbery and Rufus McCain, #AZ 267, ninety–nine years for kidnapping and bank robbery, quickly scrambled down the island cliffs to get to the bay.

For a moment the escape siren mingled with the foghorn and caused confusion. Suddenly everyone was awake. Esther Faulk got up with her husband. George Steere was awakened. The Roses were up. Later, Joyce Rose Ritz and her mother walked outside for a peek at all the excitement.

Officer Ernest Padgett was on patrol that night, armed with a .45 calibre Army automatic. It was foggy, he recalled later, and when the siren sounded he telephoned the Control Center and got word of the missing five men. Suddenly his little automatic felt like a toy. Warden Johnston was up, of course, and he remembered that the fog was as thick as a "mass of wool." Joyce Ritz and the Faulks remembered it being a clear night, at least on some parts of the island. Alec Klineschmidt, an elderly man when interviewed, insisted it had been foggy. "You could hear the tin cans rattle," he said, recalling his most vivid memory of the shooting down at the beach. Prisoners there were trapped between guards shooting from the parade ground and from the island boat.

All five scattered when the firing began. Stamphill and Barker, Stamphill later said, were pinned behind some rocks. Barker peeked up and was shot in the forehead. Stamphill was eventually released from the federal system and lived in the Midwest. He said that Barker turned around and warned him not to get up, then talked for what seemed like an hour before he lost consciousness.

While this occurred, Officer Faulk and Deputy Warden Ed Miller moved down a trail that led to the shore. They waded into the water and, suddenly, behind them, Martin accidentally fell down the embankment. Startled, Faulk later chuckled about the "capture." Like other prisoners, Martin had removed his clothing to make tie strips for the raft they were trying to build. The two officers escorted the naked, cold, and humiliated man through the parade ground up to the prison.

The still-conscious Barker, and Stamphill, wounded in the knees, were soon loaded onto a dinghy behind the island boat, and dragged to the dock on the other side of the island. This time, the guards had clearly won. (It was a dubious victory, however. Officials hadn't retooled the soft cell bars in segregation as they had the other cell fronts. Nor had an officer be permanently assigned there.)

Win or lose, however, events in these years sealed the reputation of Alcatraz as "escape proof" and a challenge for prisoners and officers. There might be humorous moments, like when Joyce Ritz and her mother got locked out of their apartment that night and Joyce tried to climb in the window, when, suddenly, an armed guard appeared, shouting, "Hold it!"

"Here I am—half in and half out—and my mother was jumping up and down, shouting, *'Don't shoot! Don't shoot!'*" The next day, they laughed about their "escape" at the same time newspapers were reporting that the notorious "Doc" Barker was dead on Alcatraz.

May, 1941

Four convicts, all life-termers, bound and gagged Captain Paul J. Madigan and a shop foreman, and attempted to saw through bars in the Industries area on May 21, 1941. Two of them, Joseph Cretzer, #AZ 548, and Sam Shockley, #AZ 462, were desperate to escape; Cretzer would be killed, and Shockley executed, for a later attempt.

This escape attempt ended in failure, largely because of one man.

Paul Madigan, captain of the guards at the time, had been handpicked as a guard by Warden Johnston to work Alcatraz. A devout Catholic and a genuinely warm Irish–American, he was, nonetheless, a tough prison man who worked every post on Alcatraz—guard, lieutenant, captain, associate warden and, eventually, warden. That made him perhaps the most valuable man who ever headed up Alcatraz, serving from 1955 until 1961—a period of relative fairness and enlightenment in the prison's history. While James A. Johnston, the first warden, had the most revered reputation, he was remote, straightlaced and old world. Times were tougher in the '30s and '40s. Madigan was a product of the more open 1950s.

A thoughtful man who smoked a pipe, he was able to measure his responses while lighting his tobacco. When he got a little mad, he gritted his teeth, my father later said, "and broke a lot of pipe stems that way." Madigan was cool under fire, though, and extremely lucky. To protect and reward him after the 1941 escape attempt, he was transferred off Alcatraz and promoted. That meant he missed two more escape attempts in which he might have been injured or killed. In one, the disastrous 1946 shoot-out, then Captain Henry Weinhold was critically shot while being held prisoner.

Madigan transferred back to Alcatraz twice more. His nickname, "Promising Paul," was a tribute to his finesse as a politician. "You'd go to him with a problem," my father, who worked on Alcatraz when Madigan was warden, said:

He'd listen, seem to approve of your solution and you'd go out satisfied. Later someone else would go in with the same problem, only on the opposite side. He'd leave satisfied and you'd

Paul J. Madigan, the warden of Alcatraz after James A. Johnston and Edwin B. Swope, serving 1955–61.

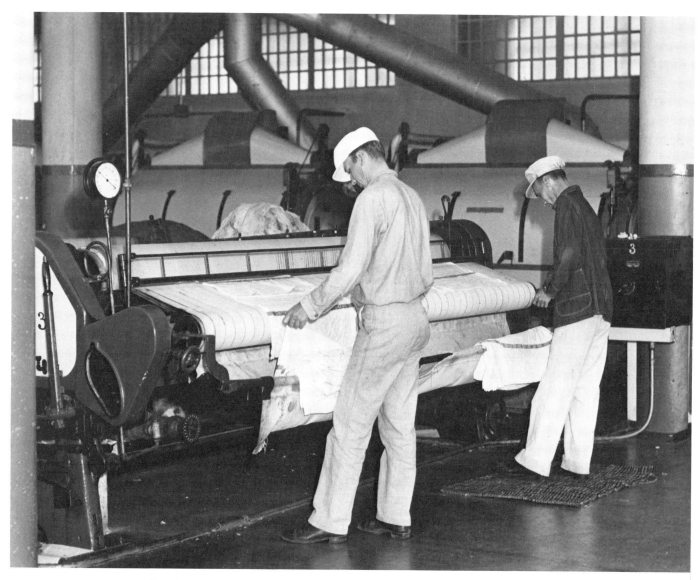

Fourth grade pay generated ten cents an hour in 1953; first grade, the top grade, earned a man twenty–five cents in 1953 and thirty cents an hour in 1959. (Long term Industrial time generated an extra five cents an hour.) Despite the low wages, Ben Rayborn, a former prisoner and later a successful paralegal in San Diego, said he helped put his daughter through college on what he earned. (PHIL DOLLISON)

An officer and three culinary inmates help load food supplies into the cell house basement. (NATIONAL MARITIME MUSEUM; BETTY WALLER COLLECTION)

find out you came out on the short end of the stick. After that happened many times, I learned to be the last one to talk with [him], and my average improved quite a bit.

Luck remained with Madigan. He transferred off Alcatraz in November, 1961, leaving Olin G. Blackwell, the last warden of Alcatraz, to serve during a more controversial period.

What singled Madigan out initially was the 1941 Cretzer–Shockley escape attempt. Tied up, but conscious, he coolly told the foursome then trying to saw through bars that they would soon be discovered. Frustrated, they gave up.

September, 1941

Four months later, John Richard Bayless, #AZ 466, jumped off the dock. Like most convicts attempting to escape Alcatraz, he hadn't counted on the bay being so cold and choppy. "He got a couple of hundred feet," remembered Marvin Orr, "and turns around and swims back! And winds up in the hole. It was too cold for him, see!"

April, 1943

Captain Henry Weinhold was surprised, bound, and gagged on April 14, 1943. Four men, Harold M. Brest, #AZ 380, serving life for bank robbery and kidnapping, Floyd Hamilton, #AZ 523, thirty years for bank robbery, Fred Hunter, #AZ 402, serving twenty-five years for postal robbery and James Boarman, #AZ 571, serving twenty years for bank robbery, got down to the shore just as Weinhold got loose and blew his whistle.

That day Warden Johnston was quoted announcing the shooting and drowning deaths of Boarman and Hamilton, and the recapture of the others.

But Hamilton was to have another fate.

Linked with the notorious husband–wife team of Bonnie and Clyde, Hamilton was tall, intelligent and soft-spoken. He had not sunk into the water and died as was reported. Instead, he swam back to the island and hid in a cave where the high tides trapped him. Hypothermic and exhausted, he left his cave finally, climbed the hill back to the prison and fell asleep in the old model building. In a comic moment of supreme irony, Captain Weinhold discovered him sleeping next to the radiator.

Hamilton is the only man known to have escaped *into* Alcatraz.

August, 1943

In the eighth Alcatraz attempt, Huron "Ted" Walters, #AZ 536, serving thirty years for bank robbery, was surrounded by officers just as he was about to launch himself into the bay, said a prison report, with "a couple of cans tied to his waist for buoyancy." For the first time, a prisoner had devised a plan for the actual swim.

July, 1945

John Giles, #AZ 250, a bright, pleasant twenty–five year post office robber, whom officers generally liked for his "good attitude," had one of the better inmate jobs as a dock worker. Over months, he collected pieces of Army clothing from the laundry. By July 31, he had assembled the entire uniform and had quietly boarded the *Frank M. Coxe,* the U.S. Army boat that docked almost daily at Alcatraz in those days. His absence was immediately noticed however, and Deputy Warden E.J. Miller sped over to Angel Island on another boat to meet Giles there. This remained the most ingenious attempt to escape from Alcatraz at least until June, 1962. Some officers expressed guarded admiration for Giles' attempt, but he lost three thousand days "good time," according to a later prison report, amounting to more than eight years, and he received an additional three years. When he got out of D block two years later, he worked one of the worst jobs—the incinerator.

May, 1946

The last escape attempt in the 1940s, began in confusion and ended in tragedy.
On May 2, 1946, Bernard Coy, #AZ 415, spread the bars into the gun gallery cage—where the only man inside the prison had a gun—knocked out Officer Bert Burch and passed guns and keys down to his buddy. Joe Cretzer and Coy, one by one, surprised and overpowered other cell house officers, imprisoned them in cells and began releasing prisoners. Miran Thompson, Marvin Hubbard, Sam Shockley and Clarence Carnes joined Coy and Cretzer in the attempt.
The would-be escapees attempted to pick off the tower guards, missed, then panicked. Thompson and Shockley reportedly screamed at Cretzer to kill their witnesses, now about nine officers trapped inside two cells. Angered because they couldn't obtain the key to get out of the cell house, Cretzer steadied his gun and fired into the cells.

Metal detectors located between Industries and the prison were often erratic, and there were ways to get items through. One man was said to have a metal plate in his skull and convicts passed items with him. Others placed small items in their shoes, shuffling through without detection. (COURTESY OF PHIL DOLLISON)

Capt. Weinhold was struck him in the chest; Lieutenant William Miller, who had already been pistol whipped, was hit in the arm. Officer Corwin took a bullet in the face. Lieutenant Simpson was hit in the abdomen and officers Lageson and Baker were also shot. (Betty Weinhold Horvath wrote later that her father, shot on her birthday, was hospitalized for months and retired with full disability. "He was never supposed to have lived through the injuries he sustained," she said. "The bullet entered his [chest], turning and passing through his right lung, thereby collapsing it, and then exiting under his armpit and reentering his upper right arm, shattering the bone." Capt. Weinhold lived another twenty years. He was involved in several escape attempts at Alcatraz, and injured in two of them. "My mother used to say that if there was an escape attempt going on, Daddy was sure to be involved.")

 No one knew what was going on in the island's residential area, but something was amiss. "We did know [prisoners] were shooting all over the place," remembered Marvin Orr, whose family was on the island at the time. "It wasn't safe to walk anyplace. They were shooting out the kitchen windows, out the cell house windows, out the hospital, shooting at the towers, at anything that moved," he said.

"As long as the place has been there," said Fred Mahan, an officer who spent seventeen years on Alcatraz, "there [were] no families hurt. In the '46 riot, inmates got access to a phone, and called up some of the people, and told 'em they would be down. They were trying to get hostages, but they didn't get out [of the cell house] to do it."

Confusion reigned near the prison as well. Warden Johnston was not a trained battle strategist. He and Associate Warden E.J. Miller overestimated on how many armed escapees were involved and loose inside the cell house. They sent an armed party to the side of the hill who were instructed to shoot into the cell house—a foolish decision because many uninvolved prisoners were trapped in their cells. They also sent a squad to rescue the trapped guards. Officers Bergen, Faulk, and Mahan were among them. But officers on the side of the hill were poorly managed and excitable. They shot inside the windows of D block, where the officers inside were vulnerable. Suddenly Officer Harold B. Stites, was fatally shot by a bullet coming from another officer.

Inside the cell house, the trapped officers were eventually rescued, but William Miller, who originally held and hid the yard door key prisoners needed to get out of the building, later died of internal injuries. His was the second guard fatality that week.

"Word came over that Mr. Miller had been killed," said Joyce Rose Ritz, who by then was an adult and at home when the escape attempt began. Although many school age children and some wives were in the city, the shooting on Alcatraz trapped others on the island. They relied on the radio for information. Joyce crept over to Associate Warden E. J. Miller's house to be with his wife (no relation to Lt. William Miller). "Word came over that Mr. Miller had been killed and we didn't know which one. I quickly grabbed the phone and called [up top] and said I was with Mrs. Miller and was it E.J? And they said 'No.' And I just hung up." Relieved, the two women continued listening to their radio.

Reinforcements from San Quentin, Leavenworth, and McNeil Island were eventually called in. Joseph Stilwell, Sixth U.S. Army commander, and Frank Merrill of the famed Merrill's Marauders offered advice. Stilwell approved a request of fifteen–pound "shake" bombs. Ten cases of grenades and ten cases of carbine ammunition were reported by newspapers to have been rushed to Alcatraz from Benicia Arsenal. Influenced by the commandos who were using World War II tactics, Johnston approved the participation of the U.S. Marines. By Friday, they were on the island, dropping grenades down a vent into the cell house—evidence of which can still be seen today on the cell house floors.

> *. . . They drilled this hole through the roof somewhere, or kicked out a window, or something [a prisoner later testified in San Francisco] but they were throwing grenades down, and the grenades were hitting behind the cells, and they were hitting pretty close, because some gas had [come] in and I had advised the boy next door to me and the boy upstairs and my partner—the cell just below me—[that] the best way to get out of that gas was to clean the commode out and breathe the air from the commode. . . I did. I had mine cleaned out, all the water taken out, a towel laying over it, and I was sitting beside it.*

Bombing continued until no more shots were returned from the cell house. Saturday morning, May 4, officers found Coy, Cretzer and Hubbard dead in a utility corridor. Each had multiple bullets holes in their torsos and heads. Coy was still dressed in an officer's uniform he had worn to fool guards. He was said to be still clutching his weapon.

Thompson, Shockley and Carnes were tried in December for the murder of William Miller. Thompson appeared surly. Lawyers based Shockley's defense on insanity and drummed up his mental incompetence but it was a weak defense. Neither man appeared sincere. They were convicted and executed at nearby San Quentin State Prison in 1948.

Carnes, #AZ714, the nineteen-year-old Choctaw Indian who had arrived at Alcatraz the year before with two life sentences, was the only prisoner to be spared—probably because

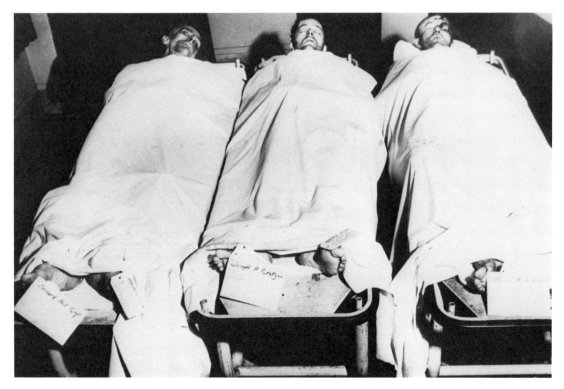

Bernard Coy, left, Joe Cretzer, center, and Marvin Hubbard, right, in mug shots and on gurneys after their deaths in 1946. (NATIONAL MARITIME MUSEUM)

Two who made it after the 1946 "Battle of Alcatraz": former captain of the guards (and then Lieutenant) Phil Bergen, left, and former prisoner Clarence Carnes. Shown here in a lighter moment in 1980 on Alcatraz, they were advisors on a television film about Carnes' life there.

(JOLENE BABYAK)

of his youth. He was given his third life sentence, and at Alcatraz he was sent to segregation for seven years. He later said that officers who had been involved in the mishap never mistreated him, but others, who had not been involved, carried grudges.

Carnes was transferred to Leavenworth when Alcatraz closed in 1963, was paroled in the late 1970s, broke parole, returned for a short time and was released again. We met one day in a fast food restaurant, despite my father's initial apprehension. Carnes had been a bitter man at Alcatraz, but outside, seemed calm and friendly.

During the next eight years that I knew him, he had a tumultuous life. He worked mostly in a Kansas City halfway house and was the subject of a television film about his life which generated appearances on national television shows. Yet he was also mugged, robbed, on welfare, and suffered bouts of periodic alcoholism which aggravated his diabetes. One Saturday night in the midst of all this, he called me, lonely and inebriated, leaving a message on my machine, "I'm sitting here, nothin' to do. And you know something? I had a better weekend, many a time, inside the penitentiary of Leavenworth than I'm having at this very moment. If I were in Leavenworth, I'd have some popcorn, or cookies, or a smuggled sandwich, and I'd be sitting at the TV with one of my friends, and be comfortable."

Carnes had spent all of his adult life in prison. He didn't know how to cope with life on the outside where there were no guarantees, no health care and no security.

According to his parole officer, in 1987, Carnes was diagnosed with acquired immune deficiency syndrome (AIDS) and was told he wouldn't see his next two birthdays. He stole a little money and went on the lam, thus breaking parole. When he turned himself in, he was quickly sent to Springfield, Missouri, where there is a federal medical prison. There he received his health care, and incarceration was a blessing of sorts.

None of the three would-be escapees were charged with the death of Officer Stites in 1946. The Bureau of Prisons promised an "exhaustive" investigation and did investigate, but the findings were never released. No one wanted to publicly chastise a prison administration nor its officers, among whom numbered at least eleven wounded and two dead, even if two men were suspected of accidentally being injured and killed by federal officers. It was not the Bureau's style to make exhaustive investigations and hold itself accountable. Not even if it meant aiding other prison officials, who would be involved in other riots that occurred across the country in the early 1950s.

Most accounts of the 1946 so-called "Battle of Alcatraz" have not dealt honestly with what really happened, perhaps because the older prison guards are suspicious of newspaper reporters. They were not reluctant to voice their opinions, however, to someone, like myself, who is considered "family".

Warden Johnston was an exemplary first warden of Alcatraz, serving during the difficult time of the depression and the World War II years. Movies about Alcatraz have sometimes portrayed him as befuddled and confused, but that diminishes him. He set the standards by which Alcatraz operated throughout its history. In 1946, however, he was seventy years old, and perhaps ill–equipped to head up such a crisis. He retired in 1948.

As always after an escape attempt, Alcatraz tightened its security. By 1946, ten escape attempts had occurred. In the next seventeen years, there would be only four more tries.

Only thirty–six prisoners got out of the buildings and down to the bay in fourteen escape attempts. The high security on Alcatraz—the fences, towers and staff— proved to be an excellent first line of defense. But it was probably the bay itself which discouraged most men from even trying. (COURTESY OF ART DOLLISON)

An officer stands guard on the prison yard wall. (Note the decaying concrete, becoming part of the reason why Alcatraz eventually closed.) "No matter how many clothes you put on, you were always cold and damp," said Phil Bergen of the yard wall. Bergen said he was assigned to the yard wall for a "solid year" because someone told Ed Miller he was tough. "You couldn't get in the pill box very often . . . and there was no protection against the elements. My face was so raw I couldn't shave." (COURTESY OF PHIL DOLLISON)

The 1962 Morris-Anglin Attempt:
The Problem

For ten years after 1946, no escape siren sounded on the island. Then on July 23, 1956, Floyd P. Wilson, AZ #956, life for murder, slipped away from the dock crew. He was found twelve hours later hiding in a crevice along the beach. He couldn't put together a raft from the driftwood on the beach and the sash cord he had in hand.

The twelfth attempt on September 29, 1958 involved Aaron Burgett, #AZ 991, who arrived in August, 1952 from Leavenworth as a Missouri postal robber, and Clyde M. Johnson, #AZ 864, a former "public enemy" from Indianapolis who transferred from Leavenworth in 1950. Johnson and Burgett were on a garbage detail with Officer Harold Miller. They surprised him, tied him up and allegedly debated killing him before they suited up for the swim. (Because the incident began near the parade ground and officers' quarters, it was potentially the most dangerous for families. But no hostages were taken; Burgett and Johnson were more interested in getting off the island immediately.)

Johnson wasn't the strongest swimmer [said Officer Fred Mahan]. He didn't get that far and he just barely made it back. He edged himself along the beach and got in a little crevice there on the Golden Gate side and Christopherson and myself climbed about half way down that cliff, then worked ourselves horizontally around the island.

There was a Coast Guard boat out there and they spotted him first. He was hiding in a crevice at the water's edge. They motioned to us and Chris and I climbed the rest of the way down the cliff and found him. That scared him so badly they had to send him to [the prison hospital] at Springfield.

"Johnson pretended to be in shock," said Clarence Carnes, "his mind had slipped:

He immediately went into this thing, even while they were putting him in the hole. But when they guard wasn't around, he was talking. Everybody knew what was going on including the guards, but what they knew and could prove was two different things.

. . . Johnson told everybody . . . Burgett had all this insulating stuff on and they each had a raincoat—with the idea that they could catch some air in a kind of turtle-back thing, and float. And Burgett put some plywood fins on his feet. He hit that water and the undertow got him. Took him down. He didn't come up.

What was left of Burgett was found two weeks later, floating face down in the water within yards of the island. Bill Long recollected, muttering sympathetically under his breath, "Burgett—ah—

He put winter underwear on, and covered that with axle grease he got out of the garage, and then put his clothes on, then his heavy 'brogan' shoes. He made swim fins from plywood, and he wired those to the bottom of his feet. These things were on his feet when we picked him up! He must have swam about thirty yards and gone down like a stone.

The body was identified by the number imprinted on his tattered prison clothes. Inmate dock workers saw the remains. My father told me later that a cloud of depression descended upon prisoners when they heard about it. It wasn't an emotional response to his death but a disappointment in the failure. Among the prisoners he was rumored to be one of the strongest, and he was healthy, so they figured he could make it.

Everyone talked about it. The officers weren't any happier about his death than the prisoners were sorry, but they were glad Burgett had failed. That was the intriguing part, my father said; his death was incidental to prisoners and employees alike. "It was his failure that counted."

By this time, largely because of the media hype surrounding Alcatraz, the numerous escape attempts, and even the 1946 "Battle of Alcatraz," getting federal prison officers to transfer to Alcatraz was becoming difficult. Sometimes the prison was dangerously understaffed and administrators tried anything to fill the gaps.

When George Gregory transferred there in the mid-1940s, he arrived on a Saturday night and was put to work on Sunday. "I thought at least they'd give me Sunday off," he groused. "I didn't even know where the cell house was."

"We talked [about this]," Dick Waszak said, remembering when he applied to the prison service for a job. "We went over the list of prisons . . . and we said, 'Well, obviously they wouldn't send a guy who just fell off the truck to Alcatraz.' I mean, that's the biggie! . . . And we put down 'anywhere in the United States.' . . . Never thinking that Alcatraz would be our assignment."

"We got the letter and handled it like a hot potato," said his wife.

"Scared the daylights out of us," he added.

It wasn't unusual for Alcatraz to be the *first* prison a man served in, after he had passed his civil service exam. He'd be told he could interview with the post office, law enforcement or Alcatraz Penitentiary. "They called me over for an interview," said Bill Rogers. "I was amazed because I thought it would be awfully hard to get a job there. The captain interviewed me and I passed [the physical] easily, and when I came back down the first thing he said when I walked in his office was, 'You want to check out a uniform and go to work right away?' "

The problem was age-old. Turnover among prison guards was high. In a 1937-38 annual

The Control Center was the nerve center of the prison. It was enclosed in bullet-proof sheet steel and plate glass. Nothing happened without the Control Center officer's knowledge. All prison counts, all keys, firearms, and ammunition were checked out here. Even the island boat officer checked with Control before departing. (PHIL DOLLISON)

report at Alcatraz, Warden Johnson reported nearly an eighteen percent turnover, and hinted that he didn't have enough men to establish a forty–eight-hour work week. By the end of World War II, a Bureau of Prisons' annual report noted a thirty–five percent overall turnover among new recruits. The Bureau faced a genuine problem which it continued to address in reports to Congress, but about which nothing was done. (Despite such public laments, annual reports often contained as many as thirty tables of statistics on prisoners, yet statistics on prison officers were seldom collected or published.)

The gap widened in the 1950s when my father, Arthur M. Dollison arrived. He transferred after putting "West Coast" on the application, feeling assured that since one of

UNITED STATES DEPARTMENT OF JUSTICE
BUREAU OF PRISONS

NOTED

TEN DAY MENU

APR 16 1962

For the Period __March 21st__ To __March 31, inclusive__

A. M. DOLLISON Estimated Population __275__
ASSOCIATE WARDEN

Day and Date	BREAKFAST	Amt. of Main Ingredient	DINNER	Amt. of Main Ingredient	SUPPER	Amt. of Main Ingredient
	PATTERN: (* Optional) Fruit or Juice; Cereal; Fresh Milk; Special Bread and/or Main Dish; Bread; Oleo; Jam*; Syrup*; Sugar; Beverage.		PATTERN: (* Optional) Soup*; Juice*; Main Course; Sauce or Gravy*; Oleo*; Potato or Substitute; Vegetable; Salad*; Relish or Pickles*; Bread and/or Rolls; Dessert; Beverage.		PATTERN: (* Optional) Soup*; Juice*; Main Course; Sauce or Gravy*; Oleo*; Potatoes or Substitute; Vegetable; Salad; Bread and/or Rolls Dessert; Beverage.	
WED 21	Choice of Dried Fruit Choice of Dry Cereal Steamed Farina Fresh Milk French Toast Hot Syrup Toast – Butter Sugar Coffee		Split Pea Soup – Crackers Creamed Chicken Giblets Fried White Rice Seasoned Fresh Spinach Hot Biscuits – Butter Lettuce & Tomato Salad French Dressing Fruit Custard Milk Drink – Tea – Bread		Baked Swiss Steak Whipped Potatoes Brown Gravy Buttered June Peas Catsup – Mustard Cabbage & Pepper Salad Sweet Cream Dressing Vanilla Ice Cream Milk Drink – Coffee & Cream – Bread	
THU 22	Choice of Dried Fruit Choice of Dry Cereal Steamed Hominy Grits Fresh Milk Danish Roll Toast Butter Sugar Coffee – Bread		Yankee Bean Soup – Croutons Brown Beef Stew Buttered Egg Noodles Steamed Cauliflower Harvard Beets Catsup – Chili Pods Green Onions – Radishes Bread Pudding w/ Lemon Sauce Milk Drink – Tea – Bread		Boiled Fresh Corned Beef Parsley Buttered Potatoes Creamed Cabbage Buttered Carrots Catsup – Horseradish Tossed Green Salad – Russian Dressing Raisin Spice Cake Milk Drink – Coffee & Cream Whole Wheat Bread	
FRI 23	Choice of Dried Fruit Choice of Dry Cereal Rolled Oats Fresh Milk Hot Cakes Hot Syrup Toast – Butter Sugar Coffee – Bread		Beef Barley Soup – Croutons Chili Con Carne Sliced Cheddar Cheese Baked Macaroni Seasoned Rapini Greens Baked Banana Squash – Catsup – Mustard Cucumber & Onion Salad Cherry Jello w. Meringue Milk Drink – Tea – Bread		Grilled Fillet of Perch Tartar Sauce – Lemon Wedges Baked Idaho Potato Buttered Green Beans Corn Muffins – Butter Creamed Cole Slaw Catsup – Chili Pods Chocolate Cream Pie Milk Drink – Coffee & Cream – Bread	
SAT 24	Choice of Dried Fruit Choice of Dry Cereal Steamed Cornmeal Fresh Milk Raised Donuts Toast Butter Sugar Coffee – Bread		Fresh Vegetable Soup – Croutons Grilled Bacon & Tomato Sandwich Lyonnaise Potatoes Cream Style Corn Glazed Parsnips Mustard – Catsup Lettuce Wedges – Mayonnaise Cocoanut Custard Milk Drink – Tea – Bread		Barbequed Spare Ribs Fried Hominy Braised Sauerkraut Buttered Zucchini Hard Rolls – Butter Mustard – Catsup Green Onions – Radishes Fresh or Canned Fruit Milk Drink – Coffee & Cream – Bread	
SUN 25	Fresh Fruit Choice of Dry Cereal Rolled Oats Skim Milk Toast Butter Apricot Jam Sugar Coffee – Bread		Southern Fried Chicken – Sage Dressing Snowflake Potatoes Giblet Gravy Buttered Asparagus Cloverleaf Rolls – Butter Cranberry Sauce Sliced Tomatoes Cottage Pudding w/ Fruit Sauce Coffee & Cream – Bread		Brown Bean Soup – Croutons Assorted Luncheon Meats Club Salad Hot Mixed Vegetables Celery Hearts – Carrot Curls Mustard – Catsup Strawberry Ice Cream Coffee & Cream – Bread	
MON 26	Choice of Dried Fruit Choice of Dry Cereal Steamed Hominy Grits Fresh Milk 2 Fried Eggs Hash Browned Potatoes Toast – Butter Sugar – Catsup		Chicken Rice Soup – Croutons Grilled Cheese Sandwich Baked Pork & Beans Seasoned Turnip Greens Stewed Okra & Tomatoes Chopped Romaine w/ 1000 Island Dressing – Mustard-Catsup Lemon Pudding w/ Meringue		Grilled Beef & Pork Sausage O'Brien Potatoes Brown Gravy Buttered Cabbage Glazed Carrots Catsup – Mustard Chilled Spiced Beets Applesauce Cake	

Holiday Activities

ALCATRAZ ISLAND

December . . . 1962

Preceding page: Part of a 1962 ten-day menu for two–hundred–and–seventy–two prisoners on Alcatraz.

This page: The Christmas Day menu printed in the Alcatraz print shop. The meal was the same year to year.

(BOTH FROM ART DOLLISON)

Christmas Eve

Christmas packages will be distributed, courtesy of the Director, Prison Industries and the Warden.

Christmas Day

Recordings and selected radio programs over two channels from 9:00 a.m. to 9:30 p.m.

Religious Services

Mass, Father J. E. Tupy 9:00
Protestant, Rev. William Anderson 10:00

Movies

December 25 .... "Second Time Around"
December 31-January 1 .... "The Boys' Night Out"

Menu

Christmas Dinner

CELERY STICKS   CRANBERRY SAUCE

ROAST YOUNG TOM TURKEY

CHESTNUT DRESSING

GIBLET GRAVY

FIESTA SALAD   STUFFED OLIVES

SNOWFLAKE POTATOES   CANDIED FRESH YAMS

BUTTERED ASPARAGUS

PARKERHOUSE ROLLS

BREAD & BUTTER

PUMPKIN PIE   FRUIT CAKE

COFFEE WITH CREAM

ALCATRAZ ISLAND

his colleagues had just gone to Alcatraz, he wouldn't. (Later he discovered the man had witnessed weeks of nightly rioting on "The Rock" and quit the prison service. Dollison was shoveled into his position, remaining nine years.) He quickly heard similar stories. Phil Bergen felt he transferred because he scored well on an exam for lieutenancy, yet the warden of Lewisburg, where Bergen was a junior officer, didn't like him. The warden wrote on his file "not suitable for promotion," Bergen said. He was given a choice of going to Alcatraz or sticking around. He chose Alcatraz. He had a long federal prison career and was eventually promoted to associate warden. Other stories were common of men who had transferred after courting disfavor at other institutions.

Drinking problems, hints of marital impropriety, petty cash scandals, rumors; the prison service is a fairly insulated society, conservative, and in the business of meting out punishment. It was part of the gallows humor on Alcatraz—the occasional story of the prison officer waking up from an all-night drunk and finding himself on a plane to Alcatraz.

Turnover was high for other reasons. A 1957 Bureau report stated that a "general handyman and trash collector [having] no contact with prisoners, earns $300 [more than] the annual salary [for] Correctional Officers." In the same report, a note at the bottom stated, "In one week five at Alcatraz resigned, each giving as his reason that he had been offered more remunerative employment. . ." Losing five posts in a week could be devastating for a short-staffed, high-profile prison like Alcatraz.

Moreover, my father observed that at times one–third of the officers had less than a years' experience in prison work. "They were as green as grass," Bergen once said, agreeing, "and the prisoners have hundreds of years of experience."

Formal training of Alcatraz officers lasted four weeks, but ninety–five percent of it consisted of on-the-job advice from senior officers. Although classes of eight or ten men were periodically held, every class experienced several dropouts, and their replacements *only* received on-the-job training. (The inmate, of course, could offer a little advice to the new man.) Alcatraz was so consistently short-staffed that captains took what they could get. "Recruitment was the most serious problem," said Bergen. "Retention was the next."

And what developed over the years, broadly speaking, were two types of employees: those who had remained for many years, gaining their experience primarily at Alcatraz, and those who were new recruits with no prior prison experience. Viewed from a larger perspective, the result caused dissimilar attitudes which converged to play an eventual part in the final controversial year on Alcatraz.

The experienced officers with a decade or more on Alcatraz, believed the prison to be escape proof. In fact, by 1961, there had only been two feeble attempts since 1946. Those guards were overconfident and becoming complacent. Other, less experienced officers, hired quickly and often trained haphazardly, had little perspective outside of Alcatraz and took their lead from their superior officers. They, too, were becoming complacent.

Both groups relaxed in their security measures, particularly in cell searches and magazine censorship. (Officers let slip through a March 1962 *Popular Science* issue with an article on watertight sailing jackets, and a May 1962 *Sports Illustrated* issue with photographs and description of a rubberized boat from which Frank Morris and John and Clarence Anglin drew information for their June, 1962 escape attempt. On the night of that escape, officers tried to find the source of unusual noises coming from the cell house roof, but didn't awaken the general population to see if anyone was missing, and alerted no one else on the island.)

To an outside observer, it might seem like the entire security system was at risk.

But that's laying blame for what followed solely on the guard force, and human events are rarely that simple. Alcatraz was an old, controversial prison, which by the early 1960s, seemed to be an anachronism to President John F. Kennedy's "New Frontier." Bureau of Prisons' Director James V. Bennett had always supported it in congressional budget requests, but by '61, had admitted that it was a decrepit relic of the past. By then of course, the prison's replacement—the U.S. Prison at Marion, Illinois—was already being built.

In 1961, Olin G. Blackwell became the fourth and final warden and appointed his staff. Bill Bradley became captain of the guards. And, in a move that astonished many officers, Blackwell appointed Arthur M. Dollison as associate warden. Although Dollison had already served on Alcatraz for eight years, all of it was in Industries. He was a business man—not a custody officer. And the associate warden was head of custody.

Like the lyrics of a song that would become popular later in the decade, "The times they are a'changin'."

Officers and prisoners, especially in work situations, or after knowing each other for many years, were usually respectful to one another. Guarded friendships were possible, but only if a third party—either prisoner or officer—wasn't present.
(NATIONAL MARITIME MUSEUM; BETTY WALLER COLLECTION)

An officer stands on the main corridor known as "Broadway," his reflection shining on the polished concrete floor. (PHIL DOLLISON)

The Plan

The concrete floor in the prison cell house today is dull and flat, but when my father accepted the promotion as associate warden the concrete was shiny and bright, the result of years of daily cleaning and polish. The cleanliness was appreciated by everyone and a source of pride to prison officers, who pointed to the floors as proof of a well-run institution. But the sheen was a mirror of sorts, and a tiny crack appeared.

Since Alcatraz closed in 1963, people's stories of what caused its closing have varied . . . one man suggested that during a renovation in the late 1950s, when hot water spigots were plumbed into the cells, a prisoner/maintenance man dropped a star drill, which later another found and used in the 1962 Morris–Anglin escape attempt . . . others blame the hanging blankets that never made it into the reports . . . others claim a vital tower was shut down on orders from Washington which allowed it to happen . . . a former prisoner fighting for some immortality or integrity, said he shut Alcatraz down, solely by supplying the major items used in the attempt—the event that is said to have closed the prison.

Whatever the contributors, the escape attempt could not have worked without the collaboration of those dust free, shiny, concrete floors.

By June 1962, Olin G. Blackwell had been warden less than one year. He was perhaps the most progressive and colorful senior administrator the prison had.

Warden Johnston, from 1934 until 1948, had set the tone and the rules. Although he was enormously respected, he had worked little in prisons outside of the top position. His successor, Edwin B. Swope, from 1948 until 1955, a difficult, contentious man, came into the federal service as an appointee from a state prison. Swope didn't have the polish of Johnston, nor the cell house experience that Paul Madigan had. Madigan was the most prepared for his position, serving as warden from 1955 until 1961. He named Blackwell as his successor in late 1961. Almost three decades had passed between the first and last wardens on Alcatraz, a time of great change in American history as well.

Warden Blackwell was a tall, rangy Texan with a languid, measured style. The Mexican-American prisoners at La Tuna, Texas, his first prison in the early 1940s, dubbed him "Lagartija," the lizard, and the name fit. He smoked heavily, liked to fish and shoot guns, and had a penchant for lolling out southern expressions. He could talk about someone being "meaner'n'a red dog," or someone having to "hunker down," idioms usually accompanied by a crack in his voice that suggested playfulness.

He remained at the medium security La Tuna institution for ten years and subsequently was promoted to federal jail inspector supervising a five-and-a-half state territory. "Hasn't anybody ever had to eat one of them damn things?" he once asked a state prison guard who carried a billy club. (Billy clubs, saps, and gas billies were common in prison for many years. Although Johnston claimed he did away with them, their use at Alcatraz was obvious and tolerated. When my father arrived in the mid-1950s they were still in use, and used even on some occasions by the then associate warden. By the last years of Madigan and Blackwell, they were abandoned altogether.) "Blackie" served six years, first as captain of the guards and then associate warden at Lewisburg Penitentiary. He was transferred to Alcatraz and made warden in November 1961, at age forty–six, one of the youngest wardens in the federal system.

Olin G. Blackwell, the last warden of Alcatraz serving from 1961 until mid-1963.

Blackwell's humor and casual style earned him many friends in the prison service. "I've had an awful lot of people tell me they were going to kill me if they got a chance," he said once with a twinkle in his eye. "I told some they'd have to get in line—a lot of people ahead of 'em." But just as quickly he was accused of playing favorites, and actively disliked by some of his staff. He was a hard drinker and island rumors focused on this and other shortcomings. But the real problem for everyone, was his goal to relax the atmosphere at Alcatraz, to move it from the 1930s into the Kennedy era. Blackwell was at the cutting edge of a new, more relaxed federal prison service. But relaxing the prison while maintaining the vigil put him squarely between the younger, more informal, guards and the older, more experienced, ones. Arguably, this allowed for considerable interpretation among both groups.

Moreover, the last years on Alcatraz were not easy. Blackwell inherited an old prison with a media–enhanced "brutal" image and little money. The power plant was old and failing and there would be electric blackouts in the remaining months. The plumbing pipes were cracking and often not fully repaired for fear they would crumble altogether. Even the prison building was in need of structural repair. The Bureau of Prisons had spent $300,000 in 1960-61, and an engineering report in 1961, indicated that an additional $4 million would be needed to renovate the prison.

While Blackwell was associate warden, Hollywood began making *Birdman of Alcatraz*, starring Burt Lancaster, adding to the public perception that the prison was a brutal institution. (The film was released while Blackwell was warden. Its subject, Robert Stroud, had already been transferred from Alcatraz by then, partly because he was old, in failing health, and the BOP realized that his death on Alcatraz might cause some embarrassment. Few people realized he was then living in the main population of the medical prison at Springfield, Missouri. Stroud died four months after Alcatraz closed in 1963, of heart failure at the age of seventy–three, the day before John F. Kennedy was killed.) "Oh, that actor," Blackwell grumbled, years later:

He got mad as hell because I wouldn't let them come on the island and shoot [the film]. I was in favor of paroling Stroud to him, you know, let him live with the son-of-a-bitch for a while.

Blackie was not bothered by the "little bitty" escape details of the two escape attempts under his watch. Twenty years after Alcatraz closed, he answered questions with generalities most of the time, refusing to specify or elaborate what had occurred in 1962.

But during his reign, censorship of the mail relaxed, as did the working relationships between officers and prisoners. New men liked the new informality, the older guards hated it. Then, after two escape attempts, the blame and criticism flew. Blackwell skirted most of the ultimate blame and remained unconcerned about unanswered questions. "The escapes that happen in any year in any institution are from human failure, nothin' more," he said emphatically. "And I can spell that out for you in exaggerated detail:

You can take the so-called 'escape-proof' jail—and they never built one—and I maintain if you put a man in it [he] can get out of it. They're as smart as we are so they can figure a way out. On the other hand, I can take two men with shotguns and a hundred inmates in an open field and keep those people there until they starve to death or they run and I shoot 'em, and I have maintained security.

The cell house was built by military prisoners from 1908 to 1912. Although it was remodeled in 1934, the corrosion on metal and concrete from the salt sea air was obvious by the 1950s.

Haven't lost a prisoner. So. An exaggerated example. No escape has ever been made without human failure.

Blackwell, however, was unable to see a correlation between the relaxation he sought and the two escape attempts that year. If his policies were admirable in the changing world, their execution by his employees was flawed.

The warden hadn't had a vacation in eighteen months when he finally left the prison, with Washington's approval, for a week of fishing that June. My father, Arthur M. Dollison, became the acting warden.

On Tuesday, June 12, 1962, Acting Lieutenant Bill Long was up in the cell house, ready to add up the morning count. Suddenly another officer rounded the corner of B block and said hurriedly, "'Bill, I got one I can't get awake.'" Long's booming voice rose and fell excitedly:

And I said, 'Well, Hell, I'll get him awake.' I walked up to the cell and I says, 'Wake up!' And . . . I reached in to tap him on the head and it felt like it crumbled. I immediately slapped at the head and it rolled on the floor!

The island phone in our house jangled at 7:20 AM with an early morning urgency. My father reached for it with some dread; it could not be good news.

"Mr. Dollison," the Control Room officer said to the acting warden, "We just found three dummies up in the cell house."

Dollison was a significant departure from past associate wardens and a clue as to how the federal prison system was changing. While some had carried billy clubs and wore their SOB reputations proudly, my father was a quiet-spoken, careful man.

He graduated from college in 1932, the deepest year of the depression where there were few new jobs. He applied for a federal prison job. Tall, thin and five pounds too light, they gave him one week to pass the physical. He didn't gain an ounce, but on the day of the physical he bought six pounds of bananas, sat down by a railroad track and ate them all. He hated bananas after that, but he got the job at the U.S. Penitentiary at Leavenworth, Kansas. It was a maximum security prison.

It was typical of his determination and stoicism. He was a quiet man, unpretentious and practical, but distant by the time we could talk. (I remember as a child sitting on his lap while he read the comics to me, but that was before Alcatraz.) He seldom waffled, and stood his ground once he made up his mind.

To understand my father, I always felt, was to understand prison men—his conservative footing tempered by a desire to help, his cynicism tethered by enthusiasm—remarkable given the maximum security setting.

His most overriding trait was his morality, which, when coupled with a calm exterior, made him seem conservative and less exciting perhaps than other men, but he often surprised me by his liberal attitudes. Although he found it difficult to believe most prisoners' stories, once, on a hunch that a prisoner was being framed when an escape note was found in his cell, he took the note and other samples of the man's writing to a San Francisco handwriting expert. The results were inconclusive, but he backed the prisoner.

He was perhaps driven as much by curiosity as convinced of the man's innocence, because inquisitiveness was a basic trait. He was an assiduous reader, with a sharpened sense of history. Learning was a lifelong pursuit. Thus it was difficult for him to understand those who lacked interest or whose logic was faulty. I can still remember with some trauma the fingernails of his thick, padded hands drumming the table as he doggedly explained mathematics to me. He had undeniable patience, but he could harden with an imposing, acerbic authority when practice didn't make perfect. He seldom swore in anger, never raised his voice, yet his fingers made those table points.

Over the years he transferred from Leavenworth, to the federal prison in Ashland, Kentucky, then after a hiatus in the Army he returned and eventually transferred to the federal prison in Terre Haute, Indiana. There he moved over to industries. He had white hair by then, and his cobalt-blue eyes seemed a little narrower. He worked nights for four years to complete a correspondence course in accounting when he transferred to Alcatraz.

He seldom talked about work, and at Alcatraz, this became more pronounced. I learned over the years, however, that the human condition, especially as represented in prison, was a source of drollery to him. He thought prisoners devoted a lot of time trying to convince themselves and each other that they were innocent, when he mostly felt otherwise. One of his stories concerned a prisoner serving a life sentence for kidnapping. For years the man submitted writs to obtain a new trial. When in fact he did get a retrial,

Arthur M. Dollison worked on Alcatraz for nine years, and was Associate Warden for one year in 1962. (PHIL DOLLISON)

he spent considerable time among his inmate friends talking up his prowess as a writ-writer and gloating over his possible release. This did not endear him to many cons, and worse, he was eventually foiled. In a retrial, he charged the woman kidnap victim with complicity, and counted on witnesses forgetting details in the nine years he'd been in prison. Despite his hopes, he was found guilty, and more horrifying, he was given the death sentence. His sentence was at the last minute reduced to life imprisonment but it did little to salve his ego, because his new sentence voided his already served nine years, and he had to start all over again. Instead of returning to Alcatraz a hero, he became the butt of jokes.

My father's stories were not gleeful. One could easily see the wry chuckle and cocked eyebrow as amused interpreters of the foibles within us all. Nonetheless, somewhere along the line, he had taken on the callousness of prison work. A small detail perhaps, in a prison mural replete with them.

Transferring to industries was logical because he was clearly a businessman more accustomed to organizing numbers than guarding people. As head of Alcatraz industries in 1958, he raised the pay rate for prisoners and changed some shops from an hourly scale to a piece-rate scale—thereby increasing incentive and production.

Blackwell picked Dollison as associate warden because of this innovation and because he knew most prisoners better than a new man would. But Dad was not a custodial man. He had little experience on the tiers. "We knew the Bureau was falling apart then," one officer joked later, adding that, today, the prison service has changed so much even ministers have become wardens.

But all this was oblivious to me in late 1961, when Dad walked into my room and asked how I'd feel if we moved back to Alcatraz. A sense of excitement overtook me. I was fourteen and in my first year of high school. I quickly realized that we'd have to leave my dog behind, that I'd have to transfer schools and make new friends, that there would be the boat again, the sometimes miserable weather, the restriction and curfews. But ever since we'd moved off the island when I was about nine years old I'd always wanted to go back. Part of it, I knew, was the sense of notoriety that I enjoyed. (Well-meaning friends used to introduce me by blurting out, "Meet my friend. She lives on Alcatraz.") But looking back now I realize it was also the sense of adventure I saw coming. I didn't know what adventure I imagined, until the phone rang that June morning in 1962.

Dad had been associate warden of the nation's most maximum security penitentiary for seven months by then. Despite the man I thought I understood, even he was controversial. "Your dad, when he was associate warden," said Bill Rogers, one of the younger guards on the island at the time, "was a very hard man." But Marvin Orr, one of the older guards, once said, "I don't think your father was quite tough enough." Now, with the warden gone for the week, Dad was acting warden. "Take Art there," said Officer Fred Mahan, "he was just learning the ropes. . ."

By the time Dollison and Acting Associate Warden Bill Bradley got to the cell house that morning, officers had determined that Frank Lee Morris and John and Clarence Anglin had crawled out vents in the back of their cells the night before, then shimmied up the utility pipes to a vent in the roof.

Frank Lee Morris, #AZ 1441, was a thirty–five-year-old with a tested IQ of one–hundred–thirty–five; he was a 5'7", bantam weight, stern-faced, chess–playing lifelong prisoner. Records showed he had a devil's head tattooed on his right arm. Morris had been shuffled from foster homes, reform schools and prisons since he was six months old.

He was first caught violating the law at age thirteen. A series of petty larcenies, house break-ins, burglaries, armed robberies, narcotics violations, parole violations and escapes had led him from boys training school to jail to prison. He served time in Washington, D.C., Ohio, Louisiana, Florida, and Alabama, until he wound up at Atlanta Federal Penitentiary in Georgia on a sentence of fourteen years for a bank heist.

The San Francisco newspapers that June made much of the fact that he was seemingly intelligent. But he was caught once burglarizing a Louisiana bank, which netted him only $6,165—not a large sum of money even in the 1950s. But worse, the booty—in coins—weighed about twelve–hundred pounds.

Morris had tried to escape from nearly every institution in which he had served time. An escape attempt at Atlanta got him transferred to Alcatraz in January, 1960.

John Anglin, #AZ 1476, at thirty–two, was a year older than his brown-haired, hotheaded brother, Clarence, #AZ 1485. Both were taller than Morris, at nearly six feet. They were serving ten and seventeen years, respectively, for bank robbery. The Anglins were loudmouthed. Some officers felt that if they hadn't had someone in control over them the entire institution would have known about the plot within two weeks. In fact, many prisoners today say they did know about it, and the Anglins were at the center of it. The brothers also have been implicated by several prisoners for inviting others in on the escape, which nearly brought everyone to blows on the yard one day. They had previous escape attempts on record but none as complex as this. The most ambitious occurred at Leavenworth in the late 1950s when Clarence was found hiding in a large bread box destined for the outside. It was this lame attempt which only got him to Alcatraz.

But there was another man whose original idea the escape was: Allen C. West. He was immediately brought out for an interview after saying, "You may as well lock me up too. I planned the entire escape." West, #AZ 1335, a short, dark-haired, wiry thirty-three-year-old inmate, serving a ten-year sentence for interstate transportation of stolen vehicles, was described as a "go-fer" by one guard and a manipulator by several others. He had been at Alcatraz twice, in 1954-56, and again in 1958-63. During his second stint in October 1960, he assaulted an officer and was placed in D block. There, he and several prisoners cut their heel tendons—a ploy used in the past to attract attention for abuse usually in state prisons, but later used to harass administrators. West's wounds were superficial and later he claimed he'd been badgered into doing it. He was assigned to cell house maintenance after getting out of D block in May 1961, and soon was working in the utility corridor behind the cells.

The ventilation grills apparently had at one time been larger.
(NATIONAL MARITIME MUSEUM)

Prisoners, as well as others, could see the deterioration in the cell house; cracks appeared frequently and cornices fell off—but it was doubtful West knew that the ventilation grills in the back of the cells had been made smaller when the Feds took over in 1934. And it wasn't even known by officials that work crews apparently hadn't reinforced the cement around the vents with steel rods or wire mesh. The erosion may have been apparent in the utility corridor.

West brought John Anglin in on the deal first, he told Dollison and Captain Bradley—they had been acquaintances at Florida Penitentiary—then brought Morris in.

According to prison and FBI reports of items found in the prisoners' cells, the quartet used hack saw blades, scraps of serrated tin, six-inch homemade chisels with taped handles, and table utensils with sharpened edges. Some officers thought the men used star drills which they had found after replumbing the cell house, but none were listed in the reports.

They worked at night, beginning in September, 1961,

digging first one hole, then another, until they had twenty or thirty and could chip away large chunks of the cement. To hide the larger and larger holes, Clarence Anglin made fake cardboard ventilator grills with simulated concrete to fit over the enlarged vents. Towels hanging down from their sinks also hid the openings.

Clarence also made dummy masks. Made of plaster, concrete and in one case, soap chips, they were painted flesh tones and topped off with human hair probably obtained from the barber shop. When two masks and two grills were finished, two men could climb out of their cells, replace the grills and work on top the cell block. West had convinced a cell house officer to put blankets around the top of the cell block. Now they could work on the ceiling ventilators.

Up there, they began making life jackets. Later FBI examination of a homemade life preserver left atop the cell block showed ingenuity. Using rubber–backed cotton raincoats, they not only sewed the seams but used hot steam pipes to vulcanize them, making them—they hoped—airtight. They also used spray bottle tops to inflate the jackets. West admitted getting the ideas from the magazines that slipped through the censors.

It was obvious that many prisoners supplied materials. Besides plaster, soap, paint, and human hair, reports showed they also used tools, a vacuum motor, heavy denim cloth, fifty or sixty raincoats, cardboard, piping, a homemade flashlight with batteries, pieces of quarter-inch scrap metal, iron wire, rods, wooden paddles made in industries.

But prisoners interviewed in the next days said they knew nothing of the escape, either before or that night. According to official memos, prisoner #1294 said he was playing his violin, heard nothing, knew nothing and had no idea anything was going on. (Officers reported later that the musicians in the population were told that night to play more quietly.) Prisoner #1415 said no one asked him for any help and even if he did know anything, he would not tell administration. Prisoner #1329 said he knew nothing, heard no noises that night, claimed he was reading and can "really get lost when I am reading a book." About twenty–eight prisoners were questioned. "You know I'm not going to talk about that," was one comment reported, "it's worth my life."

Two other prisoners were also found to have holes drilled around their vents, one with thirty–one holes. Both denied involvement, and one said he would take a lie detector test if it were given by someone not connected with the U.S. Government.

According to both FBI and prison reports, West claimed they built a 6' by 14' raft out of prison raincoats, with fifteen-inch pontoons around the edge and underneath, as well as four life preservers. If they built a pontoon raft, it was a second raft; another, a partially

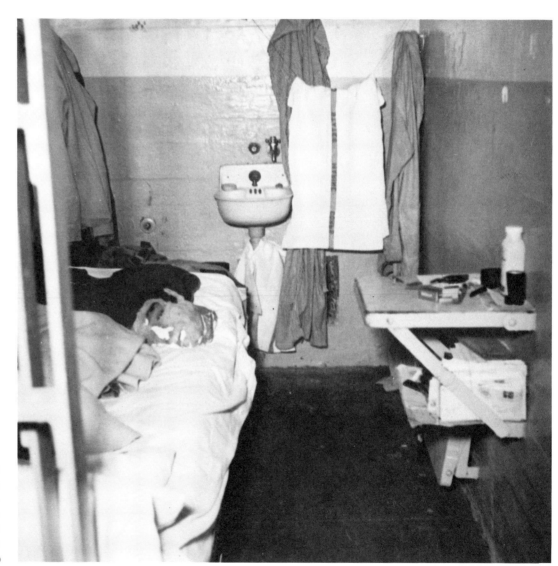

The masks made by Clarence Anglin were large but lifelike. This photo, taken on June 12, shows one on the bed and towels hanging from the sink which concealed the ventilator opening to the utility corridor. Once in the corridor, the men climbed the pipes to the cell house roof. (NAT'L MARITIME MUSEUM)

completed rubber raft approximately 6' by 2' with a wooden valve, was left behind on top of cell block B. West said they inflated the raincoat raft they had taken using a musical instrument called a concertina.

The three slipped out of the cell house on Monday, June 11, after 9:30 PM.

West never saw them again. He claimed his fake grill had been cemented so tight he was unable to loosen it that night, but he repeatedly acknowledged fear of the water.

He told Dollison, Bradley and later Blackwell and FBI agents that Morris had planned to go north to Angel Island, eventually to Marin County, where they were to have robbed a hardware store for guns, clothes and money, then stolen a helicopter for a planned getaway to a desert somewhere. Morris had read about helicopters and thought he could pilot one. They had also discussed digging a hole in the desert big enough to hide a truck, where they would hide for a month until the heat wore off.

Such a plan, my father commented wearily later that night, would have left a trail as thick as blood.

"Good Lord!" said Jean Long to my mother and me that Tuesday morning when she came to our house. "Billy was on the parade ground until 9:30 last night."

A shudder went up my spine. It had been a balmy evening June 11th when the trio left their cells and climbed down the roof to the shoreline. A large group of us kids had played a late game of baseball on the parade ground just down from the cell house.

The next morning I awoke to an unfamiliar sound of the escape siren. My father had already left for up top and mother and I did the obligatory search of our house and basement. The island was still; for a while it seemed like a ghost town.

Jean Long crept along 64 building trying to get back to her apartment, she told me later. She remembered the stillness being punctured by fright when she rounded the corner of the building and ran headlong into a man. "Scared the you-know-what out of both of us!" she said, laughing.

LuAnne Freeman worked on the mainland that Tuesday, where she could see Alcatraz from her window. "I was sitting at my desk and the mailman came through and said, 'Some of your neighbors took off this morning,' and I said, 'Sure they did.' I assumed he was talking about San Quentin. But he said, 'Call out there and see.' Well I finally got the island. I threatened to swim if they didn't send the boat for me. I wanted to know where the kids were!"

"My wife was working at the time and the kids hadn't left for school yet. I was worried about them," said Fred Freeman, who had already been assigned up top:

> *The first chance I got I called down to the house and told them to go next door. I didn't have time to worry. When they told me they were all right I knew the inmates hadn't been at the house.*

Doreen and Mike Pitzer had been driving from McNeil Island, Washington, with their parents when they arrived on Alcatraz in the midst of the crisis that Tuesday. Their father had just been transferred from the medium security institution where they'd grown up. "We couldn't have arrived on a worse day!" Doreen said:

> *We got off the boat and walked to the waiting room. Billy Rogers was hanging over the balcony of 64 building, looking [at us]. Remember how the kids used to scope out the other kids?! [She laughed.] I remember clearly, they had blood-hounds on the dock—maybe three of them. I remember that baying. I'd never seen bloodhounds until then. I kept thinking, 'I don't know about this!'*

"My kid and I were out fishing in Lake Berryessa," Warden Blackwell said many years later, "and I saw this boat comin' straight at us across the lake:

> *And I says, 'Uh-oh, we got problems' and the kid could see that too, and we started reelin' in and puttin' our gear together. And sure enough the man that run the boat dock pulled up and said, 'I don't know what the problem is but they want you to call Alcatraz right away.'*

"As soon as they hollered for me," said Officer Virgil Cullen later, "I ran up there and asked Captain Bradley, "What happened, they go out the top?" Bradley was a stocky, friendly man who had been on Alcatraz just a short time from Leavenworth Penitentiary. He was said to have commented many times on his skepticism of Alcatraz' reputation for housing the nation's worst prisoners. Although he was well-liked—not always good in a captain of the guards—and respected by some of his officers, others thought he didn't run a tight enough operation. The question had to have been a disconcerting one for Bradley.

"And he says, 'Yeah, how'd you know?' "
"And I said, 'Them damn mattress covers.' He just looked at me and grinned:

I had been working the day or so before that, and I jumped on the lieutenant about putting blankets all around the top of the cell house. I asked him why, because I could not see the inmate working up there. He said, 'That's all right. They're painting up there and I don't want the paint to come downstairs.' I'd say there were maybe thirty–forty blankets up there.

Despite the fantastic attention to detail by West, Morris and the Anglin brothers, this escape attempt would have been impossible without a corresponding number of oversights by officers and administrators.

The officer supervising West locked him into the utility corridor without direct control; this was a minor security breach at Alcatraz and rested heavily on the prevalent feeling that the island was an "escape proof" bastion, and that West could do no harm in there.

Secondly, each of the four cells had been shaken down in April and again in June without detection of the fake grill panels or significant contraband. Moreover, the night of the escape, officers heard noises that one described as sounding as if someone had hit an empty five gallon oil drum with the palm of the hand. A preliminary check with the cell house intercom system and a search of the hospital on the second floor of the cell house revealed nothing, and the officer returned to the Control Center to make out his report. The report did not state that he checked outside the building, or alerted the tower officers, however.

It was, of course, the sound of the ventilator cap on the roof being knocked open. In a strict custodial atmosphere such a noise would have initiated a stand-up count. Blackwell laid blame on his lieutenants and officers "who go around making security checks and tickin' bars," protesting, "and again, the relaxed attitude had nothing to do with that

FBI WANTED poster of John Anglin. Although John was the older of the two brothers, Clarence was thought to be the leader of the two.

(ART DOLLISON)

type of performance."

Most importantly, however, at least two officers, a lieutenant and a cell-house-in-charge gave in to the argument that blankets hung at the top of the cell block were needed to keep dust and paint chips from falling onto the clean, shiny, concrete floor. (Various prisoners may have aided the ploy by complaining of paint chips falling onto their cell beds.) Because of this major security breach, at least two prisoners were able to leave their cells nightly, over a period of two months, to work on top of cell block B, hidden by blankets, while guards continuously counted their masks.

Blackwell talked about the blankets; every officer and prisoner who was on Alcatraz in 1962, and who was interviewed mentioned the blankets as an obvious component of the attempt. (Estimates varied from a half a dozen hung to thirty or forty.) Yet, in personally signed escape activity reports in my possession, from officers and lieutenants to the captain, from the captain to the associate warden, from the associate warden to the warden, from the warden to the Bureau, the summary report by BOP Assistant Director Fred T. Wilkinson, as well as FBI reports, no mention was ever made of the blankets. If one were to rely on the reports alone, it would appear as if the blankets had never existed.

It seemed, said Wilkinson, who supervised the investigation, that security had come to rest on image instead of fact. But that assumes that the Bureau was entirely blameless, which it wasn't.

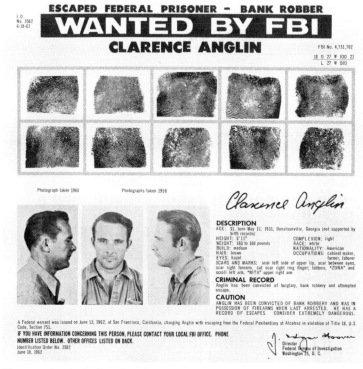

Clarence Anglin had a talent for making the face masks and fake cardboard grills which hid their activities. (ART DOLLISON)

I.O.
No. 3584
6-18-62

ESCAPED FEDERAL PRISONER
WANTED BY FBI
FRANK LEE MORRIS

FBI No. 2,157,606

22 M 9 U 100 12
L 1 U 000

ALIASES: Carl Cecil Clark, Frank Laine, Frank Lane, Frank William Lyons, Frankie Lyons, Stanley O'Neal Singletary, and others

Photographs taken 1960

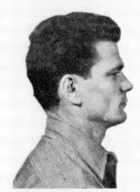

Frank Lee Morris

DESCRIPTION
AGE: 35, born September 1, 1926, Washington, D. C.
HEIGHT: 5' 7½"
WEIGHT: 135 pounds
BUILD: medium
HAIR: brown
EYES: hazel
COMPLEXION: ruddy
RACE: white
NATIONALITY: American
OCCUPATIONS: car salesman, draftsman, painter
SCARS AND MARKS: numerous tattoos including devil's head upper right arm, star base of left thumb, "13" base of left index finger

CRIMINAL RECORD
Morris has been convicted of burglary, larceny of an automobile, grand larceny, possession of narcotics, bank burglary, armed robbery and escape.

CAUTION
MORRIS HAS BEEN REPORTED TO BE ARMED IN THE PAST AND HAS A PREVIOUS RECORD OF ATTEMPTED ESCAPE. CONSIDER EXTREMELY DANGEROUS.

A Federal warrant was issued on June 13, 1962, at San Francisco, California, charging Morris with escaping from the Federal Penitentiary at Alcatraz in violation of Title 18, U.S. Code, Section 751.

IF YOU HAVE INFORMATION CONCERNING THIS PERSON, PLEASE CONTACT YOUR LOCAL FBI OFFICE. PHONE NUMBER LISTED BELOW. OTHER OFFICES LISTED ON BACK.

Identification Order No. 3584
June 18, 1962

J. Edgar Hoover
Director
Federal Bureau of Investigation
Washington 25, D. C.

Rumors had circulated since the 1930s that Alcatraz would soon close. In 1945, when Clarence Carnes arrived, he was told not to get used to the place because they were going to close it. In 1953, when my father arrived, he was told not to unpack his furniture. By the summer of 1962, however, everyone knew these rumors were true. (PHIL DOLLISON)

The Controversy

Money was the problem. Alcatraz had always been financially strapped, despite—perhaps because of—its costliness. In January 1962, BOP Director Bennett said that while other institutions needed $5.27 a day per prisoner, Alcatraz needed $13.81. Everything there took more money. While most prisons required $4 per day per prisoner for security, at Alcatraz security cost $9.69. Food costs were higher, transportation was higher, and even water, which had to be barged from the mainland, was an added expense.

Alcatraz business managers sometimes used ingenious methods to make ends meet. One former business manager, who wanted anonymity, combed military surplus property sales for items. One year he purchased the "slop chests" from twenty–one ships, thus salvaging enough tooth paste and shaving cream to get Alcatraz through the year.

The paucity of money also hurt the officer corps on Alcatraz, who were largely regarded by the Bureau—in theory as well as practice—as the least important component of the prison, third behind prisoners and administration. "Basically you were assigned to a post with an experienced officer who told you to read the post orders and then ask questions," said one officer. "And that was training. They gave you a big set of keys and said, 'Don't lose 'em.'" Officers learned mostly from good senior officers.

"The brass from Washington weren't interested in the feelings of the guards," George Gregory explained. "They *were* interested in the feelings of the inmates because they wanted to keep them quiet."

Even Blackwell cited a lack of officer training due to poor funding. "From the Bureau on down, [they] took the attitude that this was the end of the road," he explained:

People there didn't need anything and wasn't going anyplace. All they needed was to lock them up and throw the key away. That was the attitude, so they didn't

devote any money to training. . . . An institution of that type needs a high grade
of employee. You take twenty thousand inmates, skim off the toughest, roughest,
meanest, most incorrigible two–hundred–and–eighty and put 'em in one little
'bunnel,' then you need some top grade people out there.

Blackwell said he didn't think the Bureau tried to direct the day–to–day operations at Alcatraz as it did the other institutions. "They gave the warden a pretty free hand," he admitted, "they may have given us more than we should have had."

Poor funding was also a factor in one other serious matter at Alcatraz that last year. A tower position was eliminated.

Originally, Alcatraz operated with six towers. The Dock, Road, and Main towers operated twenty–four hours. The Hill, Model Roof, and Power House towers operated only during daylight hours when prisoners were out of their cells.

To save expenses, and with Washington's approval, Warden Swope closed the Main and Power House sites in the early 1950s. The Main Tower, on top of the cell house, would have been line–of–sight patrol during the 1962 Morris-Anglin escape attempt, but it had long since been abandoned.

That left four towers, only two of which operated twenty–four hours—the Dock and Road towers. "You couldn't operate the prison without those two," said Bergen. But in 1962, Blackwell allegedly closed the Road tower at night, reducing night surveillance.

Washington had approved the dismantling of tower positions in other prisons before, and subsequent escapes were the result, officers have said. It happened at both Lewisburg and Leavenworth. Despite that, and even though Bennett knew the physical plant at Alcatraz was badly deteriorated, the Bureau allowed the elimination of a tower.

"Two tower—the Road tower—was not manned at night," said Officer Levinson. "Sure it was crazy . . ." He never knew why it was closed, but he had a theory—like everyone.

"The Road Tower was shut down during the administration of Blackwell and Bradley," Bill Rogers said emphatically. "It was shut down to conserve personnel. The inmates weren't supposed to know it, but of course they did."

"Number Two tower was shut down before the Morris-Anglin escape," said Officer Fred Freeman.

"There was a lot of controversy over that," said officer Ken Blair.

"Those were quite pertinent to the operations," Blackwell said many years later about the Road tower and the so-called "Kitchen cage," which was manned when the culinary inmates were out of their cells. Some officers also said that they thought that position was shut down the last months, thus aiding John Paul Scott and Darl Parker in their December 1962 attempt—the last escape attempt in Alcatraz history. " I couldn't quite visualize us cutting down on 'em" Blackwell said. "Maybe we did, I can't say whether we didn't." When queried as to whether Captain Bradley had shut down the tower, or had urged him to do so, Blackwell said curtly, "*Bradley* wouldn't have had any authority to close down a tower. *I* could have ordered the closing of a tower, but not *Bradley*."

"'Blackie' told me he received a letter from Washington," Dollison said years after 1962. "I didn't see it...I guess they hadn't decided whether to shut down the island or not, and they were still looking for ways to cut down on expense ... But I remember Blackie talking about it. Before it was shut down. He wanted to know what I thought about it."

When interviewed, Blackwell was asked if Washington had approved in writing the elimination of tower positions.

"No," he said.

Then why are officers now saying a tower position was shut down?

"I just couldn't tell you. I wouldn't have the slightest idea," he said.

He was asked if he ordered their elimination.

"To my knowledge I did not," he said. "I can't visualize any compensation [for] the shut down of towers, because we needed all the security we could get . . . I have to qualify everything by saying it's been a long time...But logic would tell you we would not shut down a tower."

"I can't understand Blackie not—" my father broke off, incredulous. *"Did he say he didn't know anything about it at all?"*

The Bureau of Prisons denied to me all Freedom of Information requests pertaining to correspondence between Alcatraz and the Bureau those last two years. Officers were unsure exactly when the Road tower went down; some thought it closed before the Morris-Anglin escape attempt: others, including my father, were sure it closed after June 1962: some confused it with the Kitchen cage position; others thought *both* shut down. One or two claimed to know nothing about it, although everyone was privy to Alcatraz' incessant rumor mill. But all of it only underlined the lack of communication even among the officer-corps on Alcatraz on an important issue. Some of those who remembered and remarked on it did so with caution. One even cited fear of his retirement pension being yanked.

Not enough substantive evidence exists to prove that the Road tower was shut down before June 1962. But, if the tower were manned that night, it's troubling that the officer who was nearby didn't hear the noise of the ventilation cap as it was popped off and fell onto the roof.

Whether the Road tower was manned or not six months later in the December, '62 Scott–Parker escape attempt made no real difference. But the Kitchen cage was definitely involved in that attempt. And it was either not manned, or the officer inside it never saw the prisoners climb out of the basement window.

Still curious, I contacted Blackwell again, this time concentrating on the Kitchen cage. "Did you receive orders from Washington to eliminate it?" I asked. "If so, why?"

Blackwell replied almost immediately. It was a handwritten note on ruled paper, and signed with his confident, flamboyant signature. It said:

> *I have a faint recollection of the so called 'Kitchen Tower' you speak of. The action-dates-escapes-etc.—Do not ring a positive bell with me—so the only thing I can offer—is use the information you have at hand—you seem to be very positive with it. So there is really no need for me to get involved. The very best in your endeavor—Olin G. Blackwell.*

The word "positive" in the phrase "positive bell" was heavily underlined.

The June, 1962, Morris–Anglin escape attempt became one of the most famous events in Alcatraz history, largely because they—or their bodies—were never found. Despite one of the largest manhunts in the history of the nation, very little evidence emerged to prove their destinies.

On June 12, a homemade paddle floating in the bay near Angel Island was retrieved by the Coast Guard and quickly identified as matching one found on cell block B. On June 15, the U.S. Army debris boat, *Coyote,* found an waterproof package floating near Angel Island. It contained nine slips of paper with names and addresses, various letters, receipts, and almost eighty photographs of friends and relatives of the Anglins. It was supposed by prison officers that men with few outside contacts would discard such a package—even to throw off authorities.

On June 21, a man, his wife, and daughter picked up what appeared to be a homemade, olive-drab life preserver off Marin County. It matched ones found atop cell block B. One

Preceding page: "The Rock" sits in one of the most beautiful and largest bays along the West Coast, with Angel Island and Marin County to the north and the city of San Francisco to the south. The 1962 Morris-Anglin escape attempt was said to have initiated one of the largest manhunts since the Lindbergh baby kidnapping, incorporating the entire Bay Area shoreline, as well as Angel Island. The FBI and the U.S. Marshals Service staked out all friends and relatives of West, the Anglins and Morris. (NATIONAL MARITIME MUSEUM)

This page: Alcatraz prisoners leave the prison yard. (COURTESY OF PHIL DOLLISON) officer claimed the yoke-type preserver was still tied, making it appear that the prisoner had passed out and drowned—his body slipping out later. On June 22, an Alcatraz boat operator found another homemade life preserver located about fifty yards east of Alcatraz.

No raft was ever recovered. The concertina alleged to have been used to inflate it was never found. No bodies surfaced; no robberies occurred, especially of hardware or gun shops, to implicate the trio; they simply vanished without a trace.

Alcatraz officers and FBI agents combed each man's prison record. None of the trio had received visitors on Alcatraz, thus for them to set up a boat connection for the night they would depart (which wasn't known to them until that night) would be difficult. The FBI staked out all family members, former friends, and what few correspondents they had. Nothing turned up. Federal warrants were issued, and rewards set at $50,000 each were lodged. FBI records stated that a transcription of leads would produce "some hundred pages of negative information and then serve no useful purpose." Years later, rewards of $1 million each were offered and there were no leads resulting in convictions.

There have been rumors and theories—that officers aided them in getting off the island, then killed them all; that Morris lived for many years in the Midwest; that post cards were sent to Alcatraz bragging of their success; that the Anglins killed Morris; that mysterious women in heavy make up have been seen at Anglin family funerals—but no real evidence that any of the trio survived—or died in the water—has ever been documented. Once they hit the San Francisco Bay, their trial ended.

It was presumed by officers, and some prisoners, that they drowned. Each man's record was a lifelong revolving door from crimes to prison. Absence of further crimes attributable to any of them seemed evidence enough.

West transferred off Alcatraz in January, 1963, then was released from federal custody at Atlanta in January '65. In 1969 he was received by the Florida Department of Corrections on charges of grand larceny, robbery and attempted escape. With his long record and two Alcatraz terms, he was sentenced to one commitment for five years, one for life, and one for three years, to run concurrent. In 1978, when he was forty-eight years old, he died of peritonitis in the state prison.

Six months later, of course, the Scott–Parker escape attempt occurred, in which Scott floated to the San Francisco shoreline, and seemed to support the theory of those who thought Morris and the Anglins had made it. By then, U.S. Attorney General Robert F. Kennedy had announced that Alcatraz would close.

The first thirty–two prisoners on Alcatraz were transfers from the Army prison. The last prisoner assigned a number—arriving on December 20, 1962—was AZ #1576. He left with the final group on March 21, 1963.

It's easy to think today that Alcatraz closed because of the last two escape attempts, and certainly, they both hastened its closure. But, in fact, the decision to close the old prison had already been made, and its replacement—The U.S. Penitentiary at Marion, Illinois—was nearly constructed. Several reasons collided to close the famous prison—its expense, its deterioration, its infamy, and yes—perhaps even the perception that it was no longer "escape proof."

The Bureau of Prisons laid blame on some of the staff for the failures of the Morris–Anglin event. Two officers, who counted dummies numerous times on two shifts were suspended without pay for twenty and thirty day. Captain Bradley was leveled with "a high degree of responsibility for the ineffectiveness of inspections, patrols and security measures. . ." My father, Associate Warden Arthur M. Dollison, who was Acting Warden the day Morris and the Anglins left, was transferred to a minimum security institution in Texas, in effect "sent to pasture" prior to retirement in 1965. He was not reprimanded for the event, but his transfer was a "bite" of which federal officers are familiar.

Official reprimands were not leveled against the cell house lieutenants who permitted the blankets to remain in plain view above cell block B, perhaps because the blankets were not acknowledged in the official reports. Nor were the evening shift officers reprimanded for their cursory checks of cell house noises the night of the Morris-Anglin escape attempt. Blackwell was not cited for his lack of leadership. And of course, no report cited the Bureau's own responsibility for agreeing to the dismantling of tower positions.

By, January, 1963, only about a hundred prisoners were still in residence on Alcatraz. Not surprisingly, men thought to have been involved in both escape attempts were still there—Clarence Carnes, Allen West, the two other men found to have dug holes in their cells, and men suspected of lying about their knowledge of escape details, or supplying tools.

Finally, on March 21, 1963, the last twenty–seven prisoners were escorted off "The Rock." A few weeks later, Blackwell left for Lewisburg, Pennsylvania, as warden.

Justice Department officials had told reporters in 1934, when the penitentiary opened as the maximum security institution, "We are looking forward to great things from Alcatraz." It's not certain what was meant by that statement, and within what context, or whether it was even correctly quoted. But among those things were a massively expensive, deteriorated prison, and a notion of security that began in myth and ended in controversy. The concept of Alcatraz, however, did not end. It's replacement prison is no longer called that, and it's not situated on an island. But it still exists.

Epilogue

Although the last twenty–seven prisoners left "The Rock" on March 21, 1963, the prison officially closed in June. Except for a caretaker and his wife, John and Marie Hart, the island remained largely vacant. Then in March, 1964, again in early November, 1969, and finally on November 20, 1969, "Indians of all Tribes" occupied Alcatraz and claimed it as their own. Basing their occupation on a little known treaty with the U.S. Government made in the late 19th Century allowing Native Americans to claim abandoned federal property, the group declared Alcatraz, "Indian Land."

The occupation was significant because it was said to have been the first time Native Americans from many tribes came together for a common cause. Alcatraz symbolized the imprisonment they had felt on their own reservations; the land they had been assigned to, where water was scarce and crop growth was nearly impossible. "The Rock" was a perfect symbol, and they intended to set up an educational or cultural facility.

It was estimated that thousands of people landed on Alcatraz during the years it was abandoned, and especially during the occupation. Not all of them had a noble purpose. Many of the buildings were subject to vandalism and theft.

During the occupation itself, three buildings were torched—the old military officers' club house, the warden's house and the lighthouse keeper's house. It's not known who set the fires or why—whether by angered occupational forces, simple maliciousness, or by people intent on burning the Indians out.

Over time, partly because of leadership conflicts and the departure of Richard Oaks, whose twelve–year–old daughter, Yvonne, had fallen to her death on Alcatraz, the occupation forces dwindled. Alcatraz proved to be as expensive for Native Americans as it had been for the U.S. Government. Only a handful of people were left on June 11, 1971, when armed federal marshals went to Alcatraz and escorted them off.

In 1972, Alcatraz became part of the Golden Gate National Recreational Area—a National Historic Park. The Government Services Administration (GSA) and the National Parks Service jointly determined that the apartment buildings were too badly deteriorated to save. The buildings—one of which was my home for a year—were demolished and the rubble remains today. Now, scores of Black Crowned Night Herons and Western Sea Gulls nest in the foliage and raise their families. Although the rubble saddens visitors, it is, in my opinion, a "rubble with a cause."

Notes

page 19: Quotes were taken from notebooks kept by officers who allowed me to see them and from my father's notes written during inmate classification meetings he attended at Alcatraz.

page 33: Letters are a part of my father's private papers, written by prisoners usually asking to return to work after a fight with another inmate had occurred.

page 42: Studies dealing with prison officers are almost unanimous in expressing their difficult position, the "man in the middle," who feels pressure from administrators to maintain a high degree of security, and pressure from prisoners to relax the constant vigilance. They often feel they too are "in for life."

page 73: Henri Young, as portrayed in the movie, *Murder in the First*, had not been convicted of stealing $5 and did not die on Alcatraz. Instead, he was a bank robber who had served in two state prisons before Alcatraz. He killed Rufus McCain in 1940, his second killing, and was paroled from Washington State Prison in 1972. Prison conditions, as depicted in the movie, were exaggerated.

page 119: A portion of a raft was found on top of the cell block. If the raft truly had been 6 by 14 feet, as West said, it would have been unwieldy in the waves.

page 119: The FBI was notified in the fall of 1962 that a Norwegian freighter had spotted a body, with clothing similar to an Alcatraz prisoner, floating in the ocean some miles outside the Golden Gate Bridge. Because the captain had no radio contact, and didn't want to return to port when it was spotted, he didn't report the sighting until many weeks later, when it was impossible to retrieve the remains.

Information on the Morris-Anglin escape attempt was gathered from Freedom of Information requests to the FBI and the Bureau of Prisons; BOP reports; memos from Alcatraz officers, lieutenants, the captain, the associate warden, the assistant director of the Bureau; interviews of prisoners taken just after the escape attempt which were among Arthur M. Dollison's private papers; news stories from *The San Francisco Chronicle* and *The San Francisco Examiner;* and personal interviews with officers, administrators, FBI agents and prisoners. The information on the blankets and the towers was uncovered through interviews.

Information released as late as March, 2000 and which is covered in more detail in *Breaking the Rock, The Great Escape from Alcatraz*, showed that Tower Two, or the Road tower, was shut down on May 5, 1962, one month before the Morris-Anglin attempt. This tower shutdown, in fact, had a more important impact on the Scott-Parker attempt six months later. Their route—climbing up to the roof and down the other side—took full advantage of the lack of surveillance on that side of the island (see page three).

Index

Photographs are italicised.

Order these Jolene Babyak books:

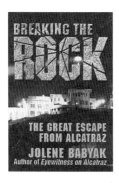

Breaking the Rock, *The Great Escape from Alcatraz*
ISBN 0-9618752-3-2   •288 page, 96 photographs $14.95•

One of the most cunning escape attempts in US history. After months of digging with common tools, four men placed dummy masks in their beds in June 1962 and broke "the Rock." Jolene Babyak reveals in her suspenseful, ground breaking new book how they did it, who aided them and how it closed the infamous prison nine months later.

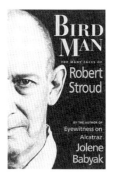

Birdman, The Many Faces of Robert Stroud
ISBN 0-9618752-2-4   •328 pages, 24 photographs $13.95•

A psychological profile of a sociopathic personality once portrayed by actor Burt Lancaster. Gritty, fast paced, well-written, with never-before-published prison reports and Stroud's own writings, with quotes from prisoners, officers, psychologists and avian pathologists, *Birdman* explodes the myths surrounding Robert Stroud.

EYEWITNESS ON ALCATRAZ, *Life on THE ROCK as told by the Guards, Families & Prisoners*
ISBN 0-9618752-0-8   •128 pages, 76 photographs $12.95•

An anecdotal history as told by more than sixty people, including prisoners, guards and families, who lived on Alcatraz during the federal prison years. Includes stories of the fourteen escape attempts.

You may order these Jolene Babyak books through your bookstores or by calling 1-800-597-9550 (10 A.M. to 8 P.M. Pacific Standard Time)